Being #1 at Being #2

Success Through Servanthood and Leadership

BEING #1 AT BEING #2

SUCCESS THROUGH SERVANTHOOD AND LEADERSHIP

by

Harry and Cheryl Salem

Harrison House
Tulsa, Oklahoma

Being #1 at Being #2 —
Success Through Servanthood and Leadership
ISBN 1-57794-133-0
Copyright © 1998 by Harry & Cheryl Salem
P. O. Box 701287
Tulsa, Oklahoma 74170

Published by Harrison House, Inc.
P. O. Box 35035
Tulsa, Oklahoma 74153

Acknowledgments

Our thanks goes to Margie Knight
for all her work on this project.

Contents

Introduction   9

1   Dad's Call To Be #1   13

2   Mom's Never-Give-Up Attitude   19

3   Cheryl's Call To Be #2   23

4   Heart Transplant   31

5   One Head, One Heart   43

6   Respecting Authority   63

7   Determined in Your Mind and Heart   73

8   Visions of the Heart   83

9   Your Piece of the Puzzle   89

10   The Rock of Our Foundation   103

11   Eternal Values   113

12   Intimacy Is IN TO ME SEE!   127

13   Run With Intensity   135

14   Taking Inventory   143

15   A Three-fold Cord   149

16   Give the Best You Have   167

17   Learning To Learn   179

Conclusion: In Weakness We Become Strong   193

Introduction

HARRY SALEM II

It's not who you are or where you are, it's what you are — what you are made of on the inside — that determines whether you are #1. It doesn't matter if you are a grocery store clerk or the president of the United States; if you are #1 on the inside, then you are #1 wherever you are.

God has called each of us to fulfill a specific destiny. Some of us are called to be *mighty* leaders and some are called to be *mighty* followers. One role is no less important than the other. The key is to do whatever God calls us to do to the very best of our ability.

We were created for relationship. The basis of salvation is relational, not emotional. God, the Father, created us after His own image, to walk with Him, to talk with Him and to fulfill His purposes on this earth. He created man and woman to walk together, to talk together, and, as one flesh, to help each other fulfill God's purposes.

God did not intend for anyone to be complete in himself. We are all servants of the Most High God, and we are an integral part of the body of Christ. We need the help and support of God and of each other to fulfill our true destinies. Therefore, as we go about our daily lives, we find

9

ourselves constantly placed in a role of serving or helping others. No man or woman escapes this role. Even a king is to serve God, his wife and family, and his constituents so they can support him.

Cheryl and I have walked a road that has allowed us to meet, work with, and at times serve many well-known ministers, world political leaders, corporate executives, Hollywood stars and sports stars. We can tell you, without any hesitation, these famous men and women are no different from you or me. The men put their pants on the same way I do every morning, and the women look just as plain as Cheryl does without any makeup in the morning.

In walking this road, we have learned through the pain of experience, and sometimes even tears, what it means to be a true servant of God, to be a helpmate to each other in marriage, to be a valued servant to those in authority over us, and to be a living testimony to our children and others. We don't say this out of pride or to pat ourselves on the back.

Cheryl and I have fallen down and scraped our knees on this road more than once, and we simply want to share with you what the Lord has taught us about *Being #1 at Being #2*. By sharing our experiences and what we have learned with you, hopefully we can keep you from tripping over the same pebbles and rocks in this roadway called life.

When we go into church services and ministry meetings, the Lord has prompted us to watch and learn what others in ministry do right and what they do wrong. If we watch and let the Holy Spirit show us what is going on by the fruit produced and learn from what we see without being judgmental, perhaps we won't have to walk that same section of the road. If we start out with wisdom doing it right, we will be that much further down the road.

A smart person learns from his/her own mistakes, but a wise person learns from someone else's. We have determined to let go of our pride and learn from our own and others' mistakes and victories. We invite you to do the same as you read this book.

Dad's Call To Be #1

HARRY SALEM II

"You will be the man of the house now. Take care of your mother and sisters. Remember what you have learned because it has prepared you for this time and for this life. Don't be a sucker for anyone. Be strong. You're a man now. Men don't cry. It is a sign of weakness. Never show emotion in public, and no one you have to deal with will be stronger than you. Never trust anyone. Confide only in your 'blood' family. You will not embarrass me or shame our name for you will lead and not follow. As I told you, all this will be yours. I'm sorry it came sooner than I planned, but you are ready." Those were the last words my father ever spoke to me.

I was just ten years old when he died, but I can still hear those words as if he spoke them yesterday. I believed what my father told me. I was the only son born into a family of Middle Eastern descent, *and* I carried my father's name in full including the heritage and traditions and all of the expectations that came with it.

My father, Harry Assad Salem, had a limited education and joined the U.S. Marine Corps to fight in World War II when he was barely seventeen years old. He was the first son of Middle Eastern immigrants. His father was a grocery store owner, and his mother never drove an automobile and only spoke broken English.

APPLE CRATE FIGHTER

Short in stature — 5 feet 3 inches tall — my father would not run from a challenge or a fight because to do so was to admit failure. As a little boy, he kept an apple crate on the front porch to stand on; so when the big boys in the neighborhood wanted to fight, he would be tall enough.

Years later in the Marine Corps, he became a golden glove boxer. This short, feisty man grew into a successful businessman owning his own automobile franchise, eventually becoming president of the Automobile Dealers Association of Michigan.

In fact, when he died, Henry Ford, himself, ordered a Lincoln hearse to be built to carry my father to his grave! (Yes, an assembly line can build a complete hearse in only 24 hours.) There were so many flowers that the funeral home staff lined the roadway all the way into the cemetery with the bouquets.

LEARNING FROM FATHER

From the moment a child is born the learning process begins. A baby is stimulated by the senses of touch, smell, taste, sight and sound. Children quickly learn to mimic what they see and hear others around them doing and saying. It goes without saying, they learn most quickly from those to whom they are closest — their parents and siblings. And so it is meant to be. Jesus testified of this in His relationship with His own Father.

> **Most assuredly, I say to you, the Son can do nothing of Himself, but what He sees the Father do; for whatever He does, the Son also does in like manner. For the Father loves the Son, and shows Him all things that He Himself does....**
>
> **John 5:19-20 NKJV**

I only had ten short years to learn from my earthly father, but he began grooming me from birth to be #1 in everything I did. He often said to me, "Son, this will be yours someday." And he meant what he said.

DRESSED FOR SUCCESS

Every Saturday he dressed me in a red sport coat, black tie, gray trousers and polished shoes with tassels and took me to work with him. Each Saturday he placed me in a different area of the business. One Saturday I would be with the bookkeeper; the next Saturday, with the finance and banking manager; and the next, joining him to visit a judge or an attorney. At that early age, I knew what red and black ink meant.

Another thing I remember my father saying to me was, "It doesn't matter what comes in the front door, it's what goes out the back door." Sometimes he would put my chair by the back door of the dealership and say, "You sit here because I can trust you as my son; and if you can tell me what's going out the back door, then we can make this business twice as successful."

THROUGH A CHILD'S EYES

At the end of each Saturday he would ask me, "What did you learn, where did you learn it, and from whom did you learn?" I always assumed he already knew the answers to his questions. One day I asked, "Daddy, why are you asking me questions that you already know the answers to?" He explained, "Son, it's because I am learning from you. You have a pure understanding of what you are learning, a simple grasp of how our business works. Because of that simplicity, I can see the business from a whole different aspect." These experiences honed my instincts and prepared me for the business world.

I watched and learned from my father at home as well. He was the head of the home, and what he said was accepted as law. He was a good provider, and he worked long hours to be successful in his business. It was important to him to provide for our needs and to create a business legacy which could be handed down to the next generation.

Although he wasn't a demonstrative man and didn't spend a lot of time with my mother, I knew my father loved her and was faithful to her. I remember him telling me, "You are to honor and cherish your mother and your wife, and you're never to be unfaithful to your wife."

PROVIDER BUT NOT A PARTICIPANT

He left the spiritual leadership and teaching up to my mother. Because of his long work hours, he did not share very much in our daily lives. But although he was often at work from early morning until nine or ten o'clock at night, family still meant everything to him.

I learned many years later that my father's strength was also the "glue" that held our extended families together — his family and my mother's. That was why after he died, the family structure crumbled, and our relatives on both sides seemingly abandoned us. As a child I was hurt and wounded by this abandonment. Years later I was able to forgive them after the Holy Spirit revealed to me that not seeing us at all was the only way that some relatives were able to deal with the pain of losing my father.

DAD'S BELIEF SYSTEM TRANSFERRED
❧

When my father said, "Someday this will be yours," I didn't understand what he meant then, but I do now. He wasn't talking just about the car business but also about assuming the role as head of our family. He was ingraining in me his way of thinking, his understanding of a leadership mentality, and his plan for passing these values along to another generation. He knew how the relatives would react and that there was no one else who would, or could, take on this responsibility. Only his offspring, his blood, his namesake could carry the weight of the family.

In the spring of 1968, my father developed leukemia. For six months he fought the disease. Then one fall day at the age of forty-three, he went home to be with the Lord.

My mother came home from the hospital in the middle of the night on November 9, 1968. My grandfather woke me up and said, "Your daddy's gone home now. Wake up, we have things to do. Be quiet so we don't wake your sisters." I went to the kitchen where my mother was sitting. She said, "Li'l Harry, take all of the pictures of your daddy off the walls for me and put them in my closet."

True to My Heritage
~~

That night as I sat in the living room where my mother lay down to rest, I realized that I was the one to lead my family as my father trained me to do. I was created, established and trained to be the one in charge. It was in my blood. I was never to take a back seat or be second to anyone. I would not cry or show emotion. I would be strong and not trust in men. I would respect my heritage and do whatever was necessary to protect and provide for my family.

The next day my mother and I picked out the clothes in which my father would be buried. That was the first in a line of events that established me in my new role as a leader — being #1. This role had been instilled in my mind from birth until my father lay on his deathbed and spoke those words that shaped my belief system and impacted my life both positively and negatively in the years to come.

Mom's Never-Give-Up Attitude

HARRY SALEM II

From the first day my father got sick, my mom gathered us all together and said, "We have to trust God." When he died, she still said, "We have to trust God." Her trust in the Lord has never wavered. When she herself got sick, she said, "Trust God." She has told us over and over again, "God is in control. He's your source, and you have to trust Him." She has provided spiritual strength and guidance in our lives from birth and still does today.

Throughout the years people often asked my mother, "Why do you put so much responsibility on such a young boy?" My mother's reply was always the same, "Because he is ready to handle it, and he wouldn't have it any other way." I'm not sure that I wouldn't have had it any other way, but I know my mother made a vow to my father that she would honor his wishes, and that was the way it was going to be.

PROMISES KEPT

My mother also promised that all of the children would graduate from high school, and we did. Important values of honesty, integrity, keeping our word and hard work were instilled in my sisters and me. We were trained to understand the value of love and family. Even today, my mother and sisters and I are very close.

My mother was determined to keep our small family together no matter what it took. When some family members suggested she couldn't provide for us, she proved them wrong. She provided the best for us even with her limited income and resources.

A Mother's Sacrifice

She would start shopping for Christmas gifts around September so she could get the most for her dollar. As a single parent, it was a given that Mom would go without so we could have more. She demonstrated to us a true sacrificial, servant's heart, and she stressed doing things with us, not just for us. No matter how tired she was, she was there for us.

When I was ten, I wanted to learn more about football, and I entered the punt, pass and kick competition at school. With Dad, when I wanted to enter the soap box derby, he was too busy to help me build the race car. He paid my cousin to build it for me. But Mom was different, even when it came to football.

I remember telling her, "Mom, I don't know how to kick the football off a tee because I don't have one, and I have never had anyone show me." Have you seen the movie, *The Bells of Saint Mary's?* Mom was just like the Sister who bought a book on boxing to show the little boy how to defend himself at the orphanage. Only Mom got me a book on how to play football, and then she got me a tee.

DETERMINATION AND GRIT

Next thing you know, we were out in the front yard. Mom was determined to show me how to kick a football. Picture this. My mom is only five foot five and a hundred and twenty pounds in all her winter clothes. She no more knew what she was doing or what she had gotten herself into than the man in the moon! Regardless, she was ready to show me the art of kicking a football!

She was wearing red tennis shoes with no socks and looked like something out of *The Old Woman Who Lived in the Shoe* storybook. She put this official Bart Starr NFL leather football — full of air I might add — on this tee, took a running start and kicked the stuffing out of that football.

Well, it looked like she had done everything right. I was impressed! The tee stayed on the ground right where it started, and the ball was airborne, for a few seconds anyway. But when I turned around, I saw her laying on the ground holding her foot in agony! I ran over to her and asked, "What's wrong?" She took her hand off her foot revealing the worst black and blue — actually purple — swollen foot I had ever seen in my life! She had broken the blood vessels in her foot.

NO MOUNTAIN TOO TALL

I helped her inside and said, "Well, that's that, I'll never learn to kick a football now." But Mom had other ideas as she said, "Don't think this is going to stop us. Tomorrow I'll wear socks!"

Mom's "never-give-up" attitude and tenacity inspired me time and again as I struggled to fill the shoes my father left for me. She never doubted my ability to be #1 at whatever I did, and she encouraged me along the way when I doubted myself. She taught me to trust in God, to do whatever it takes, to keep my word, to love my family above all else, to respect my heritage and to never, never give up. Those values became an integral part of my belief system that shaped my life. In the trials that lay ahead even in the darkest of times, I believe they saved my family from destruction and even death.

Cheryl's Call To Be #2

CHERYL SALEM

It's hard for me to think of a time when I didn't see myself as #1. I don't say this in any prideful way. It just seemed to be the way God meant for it to be. Even as a small child I was always a "let's get it done" type of person. It was just second nature for me to take the lead. I accepted it and I was comfortable in that role.

My family loved gospel music; and when we began singing in various churches, I was always the one who stepped out to do the introductions and most of the talking. My sister and brothers just expected it of me.

BOLD FAITH

When I was eleven and was recovering from a terrible car wreck that left me scarred and crippled, the boldness of my faith in God pulled me through. I told everyone who would listen, and even some who wouldn't, that God was going to heal me.

There were many who doubted, but God did what He said He would and gave me a new bone in my leg where there had been only a crushed mess. Six years later He completed the healing and miraculously grew out my short leg two inches to match the right one so I was no longer a cripple. My faith grew, and so did my determination and boldness to share the gospel with others.

Through all of this, I learned a lot from my mother about how to face adversity with strength and determination. After the car accident when all four of her children were in the hospital and two were in danger of dying, she just smiled and assured us, "We'll make it through this." She stayed strong and positive through it all and never cried in front of us. During my long recovery, she encouraged me to be all I could be despite the limitations of my physical body.

Being Miss America placed me in a position of being perceived as #1, though I saw it as a way to serve the Lord and reveal His glory to others. When God sent me out into ministry, I traveled primarily alone doing women's conferences, conventions and church services. Even after Harry and I were married, my ministry was still solo since I traveled while Harry worked and fulfilled his role with the Roberts' ministry and Oral Roberts University.

Separate Callings?

❧

Harry had his calling and I had mine. They were different and separate callings after all. For many years it was just God and me. I accepted it that way, but in my heart I knew God had a calling on Harry's life for ministry, and I wanted him to join me.

I believe that God has given me many gifts and talents and prepared me to take a leadership role to teach others how to walk in faith. As I look back, I now see that many of the painful events of my childhood and early adult years caused me to rise up in faith and forged my belief system that IN CHRIST I could overcome whatever adversities came my way.

However, I also know that painful events can negatively impact our belief systems. My past definitely challenged my beliefs and caused me to become driven by personal performance, unable to trust the one person in whom I should have put my trust — Harry, my husband.

MISGUIDED BELIEFS

God had some hard lessons to teach Harry and me about *being #1 at being #2*. We loved the Lord and purposed in our hearts to serve Him, but some of the ways in which we had handled the pain, problems and losses in our lives, or in some cases had not handled them, had caused portions of our belief systems not to be in line with God's truth. Because of this we struggled during the first eight years of our marriage and barely held at bay the strife and contention caused by the baggage of false truths we were carrying from our pasts.

A belief system is what we perceive — think or choose to believe — to be truth. Our belief system or body of truth is formed starting at birth by what we learn from our parents and others and from our experiences in life.

Notice, I said what we "perceive" to be the truth. In reality not everything we come to believe is necessarily truth. Through strongholds of pride, which can be built up and passed on from generation to generation, and through judgments we make about people in our lives, bondages are formed which prevent us from seeing the truth as it really is.

Jesus said in John 14:6 NKJV, **I am the way, the truth, and the life. No one comes to the Father except through Me.** There are times when we must let go of our pride, submit our belief systems to Jesus and ask Him to reveal to us where we are wrong. Then we must admit we are wrong, accept what He shows us to be the truth and be willing to change what we have been believing and doing. We must accept responsibility for our responses to life's good and bad experiences. Only then can we walk in the freedom of truth.

DECEIVED BY PRIDE
◦◦

Here's a real nugget of truth. People who are deceived don't know they are deceived. I had walked with God all of my life. I knew the Word and was rooted and grounded in it. I had the faith to receive healing and miracles. I traveled all over the world teaching others about the truth of the Word, and yet I was deceived.

Even with all the terrible things I had experienced in my life, I saw myself as being #1; and I know God saw me as #1, too. However, I did not realize I had built up a stronghold of pride to protect myself from the pain of any more losses in life.

I focused on winning, not losing, in every battle of my life which isn't in itself bad. Where I was in error was in be-lieving I had to drive myself even to the point of mental, physical and spiritual exhaustion in the name of doing something for God.

Perfectionism and performance became my gods as I tried to gain "approval" from God and from other people.

(Harry insisted this was reinforced by the Miss America scene, and he's right though I didn't recognize it at the time.)

I thought I was the only one who could do what I was doing, and I didn't even trust God to do it. Of course, I convinced myself God was telling me it was His calling on my life, as I traveled to save the world for Jesus and tried to be a wife and Super Mom all at the same time.

BLINDED BUT NOW I SEE!

It took many lessons from the Lord before I finally saw the truth with revelation in my heart. I remember God speaking to me one day as I was reading and meditating on the Book of Genesis. God said to me, "Did you notice what day of the week man was created?" I said, "Yes, the sixth day." He said, "Notice it was at the end of the sixth day. I made all of creation before I made you (man) because I didn't need you, I wanted you."

He then showed me this powerful nugget of truth. He said, "On the seventh day I rested and you did too. But it wasn't the seventh day to you. You were only created at the end of the previous day. It was your first full day on earth. I created you to rest in and with Me — not to toil and strive and exhaust yourself — but to rest in Me."

GOD JUST WANTED ME!

What a revelation to my driven mentality that God didn't NEED me, He just WANTED me! And the whole world wouldn't fail if I didn't kill myself trying to save it! Boy! Was

I ever wrong, deceived, stupid! I wasn't trusting God to be God. I thought I had to save the world all by myself!

Another stronghold I had erected in my life was one of rebellion to my husband's authority in our home. I believed I was a loving and submissive wife. I tried so hard to do what Harry wanted, but I was torn with my responsibility to fulfill what I perceived as God's calling in ministry as well. I had my spirit of performance and approval confused as my calling.

What a mess! I didn't realize I was usurping Harry's rightful place as the spiritual head of our home. I was so strong in my teaching gifts and in my faith that he was intimidated by the anointing.

Harry's mother had assumed the role of teaching his sisters and him about God, and so he believed that it was my role to teach our children. We went to church together most of the time, but he expected me to provide the spiritual guidance and prayer covering in the family.

STANDING IN THE WAY!

✑

I knew that I knew the Word; and, unknowingly, I wasn't *really* willing to trust him with that spiritual headship role anyway. I was standing in his way although at that time Harry wasn't fighting me for the spot. God decided it was time to make some changes in me and in Harry.

In 1992 my perfect world began to crumble. In July Harry and I lost our third son to a miscarriage. It was especially difficult because I had been so busy that summer traveling for my own ministry and also doing crusades with Richard and Lindsay Roberts.

Within two months I was pregnant again and still traveling. In November another threat of miscarriage sent me to bed for the remaining seven months of this pregnancy. I was like a caged King Kong until God finally got my attention, and I submitted to His love and acceptance and His rest.

REFINER'S FIRE

With the birth of our precious daughter, Gabrielle, in May of 1993, our testing and refining was still not finished. Gabrielle's diagnosis of sleep apnea (the condition which causes crib deaths) meant many sleepless nights.

I was back on the road again ministering, and within three months my crumbling world totally crashed. My body was in a state of exhaustion with multiple stress-induced problems and a chemical imbalance in my brain which caused depression. Over the next eighteen months I had to let God be God and put my trust completely in Him and in Harry.

This was a life and death battle. I had believed a lie, and God was in the business of teaching me the truth. The strongholds of pride and rebellion had to be torn down.

Now I can walk in freedom knowing that God loves me with an unconditional love, my strength is in Him alone, and I can trust Him with my very life and breath. I also learned to trust my precious Harry to provide the spiritual covering over me and our family. I can freely enjoy my rightful (#2) position in our home and our ministry and still be the woman God has called and created me to be.

Heart Transplant

HARRY SALEM II

For almost twenty-five years I saw the world through the eyes of a ten-year-old child. I spoke as a child. I understood as a child. I thought as a child, and what I saw was in a mirror dimly. I was living in the shadow of my father's charge to be the man of the family and to be #1 — strong, unemotional, trusting no one, a leader, not a follower.

If you had asked me if I was thinking or acting as a child all those years, I probably would have punched you in the nose. That's how the old Harry would have reacted to such a question before he came face to face with the TRUTH in that mirror and made the decision to put away childish things.

If some of the words you have just read sound familiar take a look in 1 Corinthians 13.

If I [can] speak in the tongues of men and [even] of angels, but have not love (that reasoning, intentional, spiritual devotion such as is inspired by God's love for and in us), I am only a noisy gong or a clanging cymbal.

> When I was a child, I talked like a child, I
> thought like a child, I reasoned like a child; now
> that I have become a man, I am done with childish
> ways and have put them aside. For now we are
> looking in a mirror that gives only a dim (blurred)
> reflection [of reality as in a riddle or enigma], but
> then [when perfection comes] we shall see in reali-
> ty and face to face! Now I know in part (imperfect-
> ly), but then I shall know and understand fully and
> clearly, even in the same manner as I have been
> fully and clearly known and understood [by God].
>
> 1 Corinthians 13:1,11-12

In 1992 I didn't know I was a noisy gong and a clanging cymbal, and I certainly didn't know I was functioning as
a child at the age of thirty-five. I loved my family and was
devoted to my multifaceted position as vice president for
Oral Roberts Ministries, as vice president of Oral Roberts
University, and as producer for Richard Roberts' and Oral
Roberts' television programs. I was serving God and jug-
gling many balls quite successfully I thought. So, why did I
have so many unanswered questions about my life? Why
was I always finding myself in the #2 position?

WHY #2?

⤥

After my father died, I strived to live up to his charge to
always be #1. I knew what was expected of me, and I did all
I could to take care of my mother and my sisters. About a
year after he died, my mom asked me what I thought about
going to military school. I was confused and asked, "What
did I do? How come you want to ship me off to military

school?" I was only ten years old. Military school seemed like punishment to me.

Mom explained she was concerned about my not having a male role model, and I suggested we find one. I did not want to go to military school, and I would do anything to stay at home with my dog, my mother and even my "know-it-all" sisters. (Notice the order of my priorities!) So, the search began.

TOUGH BUT TENDER

One day while watching television a commercial came on showing a huge man sitting in a chair sewing. As I watched, I recognized this big man. I said, "Mom, look. It's Rosie Grier. He's sewing!" Mom told me he wasn't sewing, he was doing needlepoint, but it seemed like girl stuff to me.

My mom was moved by this huge, tough, former NFL football player, who was secure enough in himself to do needlepoint on national TV. She pointed out that Rosie would be a great role model for me — tough but tender. So, Rosie it was! Now I had a role model that my mom thought was cool, and I was off the hook from military school. YES!

I followed Rosie's career and life. I began to play football, basketball, baseball, any and all sports. Actually, my dad had gotten me started in sports, but now that my role model was a famous football player, sports became a mainstay in my life.

SPORTIN' A 'TUDE!

I played sports with AN ATTITUDE, which carried over into my life. My mother had moved the family to Cocoa

Beach, Florida. I was not happy at being uprooted from Michigan, and I made sure that if I wasn't happy, no one else was going to be happy either.

I got into numerous scrapes on the athletic field. In one football game I had 150 yards in penalties. In one baseball game the pitcher hit me with a ball behind my ear and knocked me out while I was trying to steal third base. When I woke up, the umpire was sitting on my chest saying, "Now Harry, just calm down, calm down." He knew if he didn't sit on me I would have been all over that pitcher. I guess I had a chip on both of my shoulders because I thought I had to act tough. Somehow I had forgotten about Rosie Grier's tenderness.

My high school counselor was a former football coach from Yazoo City, Mississippi. He was a real tough redneck, a southern "good old boy." One day he said to me, "Boy, if you don't get that chip off your shoulder, you ain't gettin' through my high school. Even if you're lucky enough to slip by in your grades, I'm telling you, as your counselor, I'm not giving you any kind of recommendation for college. Do you understand?"

I heard what he said, and he made me mad enough to prove him wrong. When I graduated from high school, my counselor came to me and said, "I never thought you would make it. I thought you'd be a statistic."

Truthfully he was glad I did make it. He had checked up on me and stayed on my case all the way through school. If it hadn't been for the pressure he put on me, I probably wouldn't have made it. He cared enough to push me, and he knew how to get me to rise to the challenges he put in my path.

I changed just enough to get out of that high school and into college. I still had that air about me that said, "I don't need to conform. I can have success and keep a 'tough guy' attitude, too." I didn't realize I would have to reckon with this childish, prideful and rebellious attitude — my clanging cymbal — for many years to come.

NEVER ENOUGH TO MAKE IT

I loved sports, but I never made it to the top no matter how hard I tried. I wanted to be a professional athlete, but I wasn't tall enough for basketball, not big and heavy enough for football, not disciplined to practice or dedicated to training to make it in professional baseball. I relied on my natural talent and that wasn't enough. My physical body and skills weren't in line with what was required.

In my early twenties, opportunities in business and in ministry opened up in Tulsa, Oklahoma, working for Oral Roberts University and the Oral Roberts Ministries. God blessed me and I achieved tremendous success.

Yet, these questions lingered in the back of my mind. How can I deal with the fact that since I was born my father had trained me to be the leader, the head? How can I live with the fact I will never be the president or CEO of where I feel I am called to be? I asked the Lord these questions, and He answered me with this illustration.

I was watching one of the carpenters at the university perform his craft. I saw what he created out of wood and thought, *Boy, I'd like to be able to do that.* I went home and tried to copy his craft and make one just like I had seen him make. Mine didn't turn out like his — not even close. Then I realized I had the wood, the tools, the drawings, the hands, the eyes, a sharp mind, and the desire to do it. What I was lacking was the skill, the gifting, the anointing or calling to do what he did. Lots of people can play the piano, but only gifted people make music.

THE TRUTH OF GOD'S CALL
❧

Finally, I understood that's how it was with my dad and me. He trained me and I had the skills to be #1 in his business, the car business. It would be second nature for me. The truth is God didn't call me to the car business. He called me to a #2 position at the University and at the Ministry, and my accomplishments are measured by Him, not man.

He called me to *be #1 at being #2* — to give it my all. When I understood the truth about God's calling and anointing, I found the peace to stay right where He had placed me at least until He changed my assignment. I was able to put aside the childish idea I had clung to that I wasn't living up to my dad's charge to be #1.

That revelation of truth about my calling did not just drop into my heart one day. I didn't just suddenly "get it." God had to walk me through the fire before I was ready to lay down my prideful "self" and learn to walk in humility and obedience so I could hear and accept that truth in all areas of my life. Only then could I truly *be #1 at being #2*.

When Cheryl and I met in 1985, I was producing the Richard Roberts' television show, and she was a guest on the show. Never in my wildest imagination could I have thought God would choose for my mate a former Miss America who traveled extensively, singing, speaking and ministering to people.

My picture of family life was the diapers, grocery shopping, two cars in the garage, have my wife make my breakfast and send me off to work scenario. That kind of life couldn't possibly agree with a former Miss America! Well, God had a surprise for me, and I learned what He means in Isaiah 55: 8-9 NKJV,

> **"For My thoughts are not your thoughts, nor are your ways My ways," says the Lord. "For as the heavens are higher than the earth, so are My ways higher than your ways, and My thoughts than your thoughts."**

The Lord showed me Cheryl's heart while I watched her minister at the University chapel service. He showed me someone who was hurting on the inside, not the strong, outgoing person who was on the platform ministering. When I shared with her what I saw, it touched her heart though she didn't acknowledge it to me at the time.

Over the next few months we met two more times when she appeared on the show. We never dated. We were both too busy, but God moved quickly, and we were married a few months later, much to the surprise of everyone around us.

A QUICK EDUCATION

It wasn't until after we were married that I really realized who I had married and how her position would affect our relationship. Quickly, I got an education and so did she!

Here's an example. On the phone one day an employee of Cheryl's began to tell me what I needed to understand about her, and what I needed to do as her husband and so on. Immediately I made it clear that it wasn't going to be that way at MY house, and I wasn't playing second fiddle to any beauty queen. In no way, shape or form was I going to lower myself to that level! I hung up the phone. Then I called Cheryl and told her to deal with this person. I gave her an ultimatum to submit to me in every area, even ministry, or pack her bags and go back to Nashville.

STILL CLANGING
❧

She did what I asked. Boy, talk about an attitude. My cymbal was clanging loudly, but I couldn't hear it. I can't believe I demanded so much, so fast in our relationship. To her credit, Cheryl has always been agreeable to my requests, because she respects me as the head of the family. But I was hard on her, not because I didn't love her but because I thought that's the way it was supposed to be. In my mind I was trying to protect her, but my selfish, manly pride kept rising up.

During our first year of marriage, my career was evolving quickly. I was promoted to vice president of operations for Oral Roberts Ministries and to vice president of buildings and grounds for Oral Roberts University. A short while later, I assumed responsibility for a 300-room hotel and an 800-unit apartment complex. I was still producing the television shows and was the head of the television department. There was no subtraction, only more and more additions to my job description. I convinced myself this must be God's plan to meet the needs of my soon-to-expand family, and it was wonderful to be needed and trusted with so many great responsibilities.

Cheryl was pregnant with our first child and was traveling more and more, which meant our time together was dwindling. Since my duties were growing by the minute, and "I" reported to the president of the University, I didn't have any flexibility in my schedule. Since Cheryl had free rein of her time, it was obvious to me, but not to her, that she should change *her* schedule. As head of the home, I was trying to force her to cut back while she was trying to make me see I was stretching myself far too thin. We were at a roadblock, but I knew I was right!

GOD SPEAKS

However, God has a way of speaking to the most strong willed of His children. Cheryl was traveling to the East Coast, and I was at a Norvel Hayes meeting in southern California. The Lord spoke to me as clear as a bell and said, "I have called you to your ministry and the place you are, and Cheryl supports you in that. I have called Cheryl to her ministry and in the place she is, yet you don't support her in that calling. If you can't support her as she supports you, then you will be standing before Me!"

I didn't know if I was going to get an earthly visitation from God or if I was going up in the next load to heaven to stand before Him. Either way, I wasn't looking forward to it.

I called Cheryl after the meeting that night and told her what had happened. I told her from that point on I would support her in her calling. God had spoken, and I knew I had been disrespectful of His plan and purpose for Cheryl's ministry. I knew I had to be obedient to the Lord in this, but I still "kicked against the pricks" many times.

ONE SMALL STEP

Hearing God's voice and responding was one small baby step in learning how to respond to others with an attitude of humility and love, but I had a long way to go. I was still seeing through the mirror dimly and following the pattern set by my father. I had become a workaholic, and I had no clue how to balance my priorities.

At home I was a great provider but a lousy participant. I loved my family deeply, but I was seldom there for them. Cheryl took the kids to school and went to the games, plays and other school events. I rarely went to church on Sunday with my family even when I wasn't traveling with the Roberts' Ministries, and I took no active role in the spiritual leadership of the home. After all Cheryl was a better teacher and had more faith than I did, and it was the mother's place to teach the children, wasn't it?

Finally, God decided it was time to turn up the heat and get my attention. He was tired of my childish ways and of listening to my clanging cymbal — my prideful attitude. Cheryl shared with you in the last chapter some of the struggles we walked through beginning in 1992. It was pain and it was joy all mixed together, losing a son and then being blessed with a beautiful baby girl. I was stretched to the limit trying to help Cheryl at home and still carrying the heavy load of responsibilities at the University and the Ministry.

A WAKE-UP CALL

My wake-up call came one afternoon in 1993. Cheryl had gotten sick a few months after Gabrielle's birth, and the doctors didn't seem to have any easy answers as to what was wrong. They diagnosed a "chemical imbalance" in her brain that caused depression. Miss "choose to be happy" was depressed.

I had never known anyone with depression and did not know how to deal with it. She was crying out for me to listen, and I was using my typical "fix it" routine. "Take your medicine. Eat something. Get some rest."

We were standing in the kitchen when she turned to me, barely holding back the tears, and said, "I wish I could just slip down in the bathtub or walk into the deep end of the pool and go to be with Jesus." When I looked into her eyes, all I saw was a dark emptiness, like there was no one home. When I looked at her body, I saw a skeleton of a woman weighing less than 90 pounds.

At that moment, I knew if I didn't change my attitude and my approach to this crisis, I was going to lose my beautiful, loving wife and would be raising my children alone. I had to understand that she couldn't "fix" the problem, and I couldn't either. She was crying out to me in her time of need; she just needed *me*. This was life and death! God had my attention, and He held all the keys.

IN SICKNESS AND IN HEALTH

Over the next eighteen months, I learned what it took to truly be an intimate, loving helpmate to my wife, meeting her every need in sickness and in health. I discovered who each of my children were as I cared for them in all the little personal ways they needed me to when mommy was too sick to do it for them. I found out how misguided my beliefs were about my priorities in life as I set aside my career responsibilities to be at home with my family and with the Lord. But most importantly, I learned how to seek the face of God and find Him always there, always loving, always providing, always protecting, always helping, always answering. I began a new spiritual journey of faith, hope and love to become the spiritual head and covering for my family.

A NEW HEART!
❧

I'm a long way from perfection, but I know I see more clearly in the mirror now. Truthfully, I can say He has taught me how to love others with His compassion and not to hide my emotions. He gave me a new heart. I have chosen to put away my childish, selfish, prideful ways and become the new man God has called me to be IN CHRIST, in my home, in our family ministry and at work.

I am so thankful for my loving, heavenly Father who has taken the place of my earthly father in guiding me and teaching me how to be the head and the covering for my family in the way He meant for it to be done. I pray that my clanging cymbal has been silenced by the TRUTH that has set me free! (The full story of Harry's journey out of deception into truth can be found in his book, *For Men Only*.)

One Head, One Heart

CHERYL SALEM

No battle was ever won with two commanding generals. In fact, one of the greatest, centuries-old battle strategies is to divide and conquer. Likewise, no country can have two kings, no corporation can have two presidents, and no household can have two heads.

Jesus spoke of such division in Matthew 12:25 NKJV:

> **Every kingdom divided against itself is brought to desolation, and every city or house divided against itself will not stand.**

Is it any wonder that the devil uses that same strategy of division to destroy our relationship with God, to destroy our families and every God-given relationship we have? He started using his "divide and conquer" tactics in the Garden of Eden, and he hasn't stopped since.

A TWO-HEADED MONSTER!

Have you ever heard the saying, "Anything with two heads is a monster?" Just think about that statement.

Countries have been torn apart by strife and turmoil when two men wanted to lead.

A good example is what recently occurred in Cambodia. Two different political factions tried to jointly lead the country with a co-presidency. On the surface it seemed to work for a few years, but there was an underlying spirit of division at work. A coup was inevitable, and the stronger faction rose up and took control away from the king's son.

God has a divine order even in the Godhead which is three in one — Father, Son and Holy Spirit. Each has His own purpose, function and authority. But God, the Father, is the HEAD.

When Jesus, the Son, was on earth, He honored His Father's authority and did only what the Father told Him to do.

> **Most assuredly, I say to you, the Son can do nothing of Himself, but what He sees the Father do; for whatever He does, the Son also does in like manner.**
>
> **John 5:19** NKJV

> **Do you not believe that I am in the Father, and the Father in Me? The words that I speak to you I do not speak on My own authority; but the Father who dwells in Me does the works. Believe Me that I am in the Father and the Father in Me, or else believe Me for the sake of the works themselves.**
>
> **John 14:10-11** NKJV

> **But that the world may know that I love the Father, and as the Father gave Me commandment, so I do.**
>
> **John 14:31** NKJV

> I have glorified You on the earth. I have fin-
> ished the work which You have given Me to do.
>
> John 17:4 NKJV

Jesus led by example. He was an example of the Father
in all that He did. Jesus has delegated authority to the
Church, and the marriage relationship is representative of
the relationship of the Church to Jesus. Paul speaks of this
divine order in his letter to the Ephesians.

> And He Himself gave some to be apostles,
> some prophets, some evangelists, and some pas-
> tors and teachers, for the equipping of the saints
> for the work of the ministry, for the edifying of the
> body of Christ, till we all come to the unity of the
> faith and of the knowledge of the Son of God, to be
> a perfect man, to the measure and stature of the
> fullness of Christ.
>
> Ephesians 4:11-12 NKJV

> Wives, be subject (be submissive and adapt
> yourselves) to your own husbands as [a service] to
> the Lord. For the husband is head of the wife as
> Christ is the Head of the church, Himself the
> Savior of [His] body. As the church is subject to
> Christ, so let wives also be subject in everything to
> their husbands. Husbands, love your wives, as
> Christ loved the church and gave Himself for her,
> so that He might sanctify her, having cleansed her
> by the washing of water with the Word, that He
> might present the church to Himself in glorious
> splendor, without spot or wrinkle or any such
> things [that she might be holy and faultless]. Even
> so husbands should love their wives as [being in a

sense] their own bodies. He who loves his own wife loves himself. For no man ever hated his own flesh, but nourishes and carefully protects and cherishes it, as Christ does the church. However let each man of you [without exception] love his wife as [being in a sense] his very own self; and let the wife see that she respects and reverences her husband [that she notices him, regards him, honors him, prefers him, venerates, and esteems him; and that she defers to him, praises him, and loves and admires him exceedingly].

Ephesians 5:22-29,33

If we could really comprehend such an intimate relationship and follow this divine order of authority, I believe we could truly experience fulfilling and marvelous marriage relationships. Unfortunately, most homes in America — yes, even Christian homes — are out of order, and our humanistic, rebellious society has convinced us that the words "submission" and "authority" are not worthy of consideration. The devil is still alive and well and has deceived even God's people into believing his lies.

Too many of our homes have two-headed monsters in them. All my life I have been watching marriages that were not peaceful, harmonious, good, wonderful and exemplary. Of course, everyone thought they were, but they weren't when you looked at them. In my own marriage during the first eight to ten years, I would never have put my marriage up as an example except for what not to do.

For years the people that traveled with me were so sympathetic and prayed for me, and, oh, felt so sorry for me. But you have to realize I was sowing discord just by the words I was speaking out of my mouth about our marriage.

IT TAKES TWO TO TANGLE!

Harry and I loved each other, but we were living in an upside down, disorderly mess. We both were carrying baggage from the past and did not know how to do it any differently. I would say over and over, "This is not all my husband's fault, this is my fault too." I wasn't quite sure *what* I was doing wrong, but I knew I was doing *something* wrong.

I think most people realize if they keep their heart open to God, He won't let them think they're the one that's always right. If you come across somebody who always thinks he or she's the one who is right and somebody else is always wrong, that pretty much tells you that person is not closely tuned in to the Father. Because the Father won't let us do that.

Maybe to the onlooker I looked right and Harry looked wrong. But it probably was because I gave a facade of trusting everybody, loving everybody, believing everybody, getting along with everybody while Harry gave a facade of being cold and mad and frustrated. So that made him look wrong all the time, even though he wasn't, and it made me look right all the time. That's one example of a two-headed monster, because I made everybody see what I wanted them to see, instead of what really was there. I was in control.

A SLAVE MENTALITY

Another example was in the area of submission. I was *obedient* to Harry in what he wanted me to do, but not because I agreed with him. Willingness comes with agreement — not just obedience.

As Harry said for the first eight to ten years of our marriage, I was the personification of obedience, but while I was sitting down on the outside, I was standing up on the inside. I did everything that he told me to do, but I only did it because I thought I had to do it to be a submissive wife, not because I agreed with him or thought he was right. I did it because in my mind I had to do it, but it wasn't in my heart. I had a "slave" mentality rather than a "servant" mentality.

Obedience without willingness is futile. It has to be a willingness of the mind *and* an act of the heart.

> **I will establish his kingdom forever if he loyally and continuously obeys My commandments and My ordinances, as he does today.**
>
> **And you, Solomon my son, know the God of your father [have personal knowledge of Him, be acquainted with, and understand Him; appreciate, heed, and cherish Him] and serve Him with a blameless heart and a willing mind. For the Lord searches all hearts and minds and understands all the wanderings of the thoughts. If you seek Him [inquiring for and of Him and requiring Him as your first and vital necessity] you will find Him: but if you forsake Him, He will cast you off forever!**
>
> **1 Chronicles 28:7,9**

That's the willful choice of the heart, which is what obedience is, not just an action of the flesh. I would do what Harry told me to do, but I would mouth about it and not always to other people. Sometimes I would just go in the bathroom and just mouth and mouth and mouth to myself.

I justified it by telling myself it was better than arguing with Harry. But was it healthier for our relationship or was it ultimately right? No, I needed to get before the Lord and get it out of my system, get healed of that rebellion. I was manifesting a rebellious spirit because inwardly I was full of rebellion.

WILLING OBEDIENCE

I know now that my unwillingness in obeying Harry came from not trusting him. I think many times a woman will rise up to be the leader because she doesn't trust her husband to be the leader. It's not because she really wants to be the leader, but because she doesn't trust him to be the leader — doesn't trust him to cover her. So she thinks, "I'd better jump in here just to make sure that I'm going to be okay — that my family is going to be okay."

I think ultimately every woman has the desire to relax and be covered, to not have to lead but enjoy following. Because we have to make so many decisions just as the female of the home, we really don't want to make all those other decisions. But because we don't trust our mate to do it, we jump in and do it anyway. Then the family has two heads, which causes conflict, friction and frustration on everybody's part. It all goes back to trust. If I trust you to do your role, then I won't try to do it for you.

Here's a key point about trust. When a woman doesn't know how to trust the Lord, she'll never know how to trust her husband. You start by learning to trust the Lord, and then you learn how to trust your husband through time. Believe it or not, love has very little to do with it. I think people confuse love and trust. Trust is based on building a relationship over time.

TRUST = TIME SPENT
☙

Harry and I were married, but we had spent very little time building our trust relationship. The years had gone by so it seemed like there had been time spent, but there wasn't time spent in developing trust.

My time was spent in building the ministry and the call that I felt God had on my life. My personality was so single focused, I didn't know how to focus on building God's call to ministry *and* to marriage. I didn't want to disappoint God and I didn't know how to shift gears.

When I married Harry I thought, *Well, he married me with God's call on me, and I know God says His call is without repentance. Since God isn't going to change the call, then Harry will understand what I have to do.*

As time moved along, I couldn't figure out how to be what Harry needed me to be and not be disobedient to God. Consequently, I was much more fearful of displeasing the Father than I was of displeasing Harry. I wanted the Lord's approval more than I wanted Harry's, and I wanted to be obedient to the Lord more than to Harry. And because Harry wasn't lining up with what I *thought* the Lord wanted me to do, then Harry had to work it out and change. Boy, was I wrong!

It took me years to figure out that the Lord was big enough to take care of Harry if I would get in the right chain of command. What I needed to do was trust the Lord to handle Harry. By being so focused on what I was doing "for God," I couldn't, or maybe wouldn't, downshift into neutral long enough to let God work on Harry.

I was driven by that spirit of approval, that spirit of performance and that spirit of perfection. Until those three spirits were completely broken off of me, I wasn't able to get into right relationship and order with God or my husband. Harry finally helped me realize he loved me unconditionally with or without the crown, on or off the stage, in sickness and in health.

THE TRUST FACTOR

The reason the two-headed monster kept rearing his ugly head in our home was because of the trust factor. I didn't trust God, and I didn't trust Harry. Now listen carefully, Harry's picture is right beside the words "loyal" and "faithful" in the dictionary, and my picture is right next to the word "spiritual."

I knew Harry loved the Lord, but he was so logical and black and white in his thinking that in *my* way of thinking, he had not one spiritual thought. Nothing in his life — whether it had to do with the children or me, business, home or anything else — was approached from a spiritual angle. Nothing was prayed over. At least that's what I thought.

Harry never took my hand and prayed with me about anything. I could beg, plead or cry, "Please pray with me about this." No matter what I said or did, he wouldn't pray with me. He would get mad and frustrated and say, "You're trying to force me to do something I don't want to do!"

All I wanted him to do was pray over me, so I could trust him enough to relax about my covering and the covering over our home. But he perceived me as pushing spiritual things down his throat with a "do it my way" attitude. It's not always what you do but what is perceived that can create a problem!

HARRY'S STAND-IN
∽∽

Let me share with you another area of my thinking in which the enemy had deceived me. I limited God by thinking if my husband wasn't going to put that spiritual covering over the home then I had to do it. What I didn't realize was that Harry couldn't take his rightful place, if I was standing in it. Besides that, God didn't expect me to be the spiritual covering. Psalm 146:9 says, **He upholds the fatherless and the widow and sets them upright.**

You may not be a natural widow, but you may be a spiritual widow. This means that when your husband doesn't take his rightful place, in God's eyes you are like a widow — a spiritual widow — and He provides the covering. It took me years to understand this. I guess I was blinded and looking through a glass darkly. When I finally saw it, I quit trying to be the head in our family.

DO IT BY FAITH!
∽∽

I could trust God for everything except making my husband be the spiritual man he needed to be. I finally came to realize I had to trust God to do it by faith — not just talk about it but put it into practice. I have told this to so many women, "Do it by faith. I don't care what they do. I don't care how awful they act, do it by faith that God, not your husband, is capable." It is not easy to walk it out, but it is worth it in the end.

God had to bring me to the point of desperation. I was sick and in the depths of depression. My mind was not myself. I didn't think like myself. I didn't have normal thoughts like I had trained myself for years to think. My body would not respond to the food I put in it. I was totally out of balance.

The only thing that was like me was my spirit man. I never felt disconnected from the Father. And yet, my faith couldn't be activated to the point that I could get my mouth in line with it. My mind would not get in gear to let me speak the Word, and it took the greatest discipline and sacrifice of the flesh to make myself pray and speak positive affirmations of faith from the Word.

I kept losing my voice for long periods of time, but I knew I needed the power of the spoken Word. So when I would have good days and my voice returned, I literally recorded my voice on tape quoting the Word. Then when the bad days came again, I would play the recording over and over.

It was at this point that Harry realized I couldn't do it myself. It took that to spiritually kick him in the seat hard enough to make him realize what he needed to do to provide our spiritual covering. And it probably took that for me to back off and let him.

SCRAMBLED MESSAGES

God has His own way of getting our attention and His timing is always perfect. Just at the time I couldn't pray and speak the Word for myself or for our children, God got Harry's attention regarding his spiritual responsibilities.

I had been crying out to Harry in a lot of ways over the years, but he couldn't hear me. I wasn't communicating in a language he could understand. I should have been crying out to God. He is always listening.

Call to Me, and I will answer you, and show you great and mighty things, which you do not know.

Jeremiah 33:3 NKJV

Jimmy Evans, a pastor from Amarillo, Texas, has a wonderful book and tape series titled *Marriage on the Rock*. He says that man's most profound need is for honor, and when a wife's voice has a tone of dishonor in it, the message is scrambled. He doesn't hear what she is saying. We need to be careful what we say and how we say it, if we want our husbands to hear us. Pastor Evans also says, "Any woman can honor a man who deserves it. A wise woman will honor a man even though he hasn't earned it, and it will build his respect for her."[1]

I believe women naturally want the right order — God's divine order — in their home. But if they try to tell their husband and he doesn't respond quickly enough, or they don't see the fruit of it, often the wife is too quick to pick up the mantle of leadership again.

I had to learn to trust God in this even when I didn't see any results right away. I had to turn the reins over to Harry and let him take the lead. I had tried everything else. I would say, "You go pray with the children tonight," but at first he didn't do it readily or at all sometimes.

HIS WAY, NOT MY WAY!

Here's another thing wives must remember. When you give up authority, you have to trust them to do it their way. At first when Harry didn't do it my way, I would get upset and think, *You should know how to do this. You've seen me do it for years. You know how to pray with the children. You're not praying the Word. You're not making them pray right!*

It was almost enough to make me pick it back up again until God said to me, "You know, everybody has a way, and you learned your way. Now let Harry learn it his way." I had to lighten up and let him do it his way. That was real hard for me to do because in my mind, my way was the right way, but I learned it isn't the only way.

I also learned that if we are really good at something, it intimidates others. When I tried to talk to Harry about taking a role in spiritual matters in our home, he said, "Why should I bother? I'd never do it better than you do it anyway?" I never saw that intimidation. I just saw spiritual laziness, sloughing off his duty. What Harry saw was the natural gifting of a teacher in me that got quick results, and he didn't feel he could compete.

I praise God that Harry now is following the call of God on his life. He has stepped into his rightful role in the home and even in the ministry, and he does a great job. He may not get the yells and hollers and screams when he speaks, but that's not his way anyway.

I tell him to focus on the results, not on the in-between strokes. A lot of people get the yelling, screaming and shouting and the jumping up and down, running around the room when they speak. But what matters is when they get to the altar, do they make a change in their life? Being a mo-tivator is a wonderful gift, but it doesn't mean a thing if no one walks a different walk tomorrow.

It has helped me tremendously to realize I don't have to be the head because Harry's personality gets results. And when it's in God's order, whether it's the right personality or not, God watches over His Word to perform it in every aspect of our lives.

For I am alert and active, watching over My word to perform it.

Jeremiah 1:12

Many times women think, "I can do it better than him," but the fact is, they weren't created to be #1 in the home. And if they're out of order, it's not in the order of His Word to watch over and perform what they are doing. The #2 position in the home is an equally powerful position in the kingdom of God as a woman walks in submission and obe-dience to His Word.

IT'S GOD'S DESIGN
❦

What most of us don't realize or think about is that God is both male and female — or neither male nor female — but all-encompassing! Just look at His character and nature. You will recognize both male and female traits. No one human being could handle all of His personality (character). So, God created man and out of man He created woman. He divided His character traits between the two. It is critical to accept and respect these inherent differences between men and women. It is God's design.

God created man to be the giver of life and the woman to be the receiver of life. Then He gave us the ability to unite as one to procreate. God needs procreation, and He needs unity. It doesn't work to have two givers or two receivers. There must be a giver and a receiver to create life. God speaks clearly of this in Malachi 2:15.

> **And did not God make [you and your wife] one [flesh]? Did not One make you and preserve your spirit alive? And why [did God make you two] one? Because he sought a godly offspring [from your union]. Therefore take heed to yourselves, and let no one deal treacherously and be faithless to the wife of his youth.**

Earlier in this chapter we read in Ephesians 5 what the apostle Paul said about God's divine order for marriage. In 1 Peter 3 we read what Peter says about God's order. As you read this, consider the personality and character traits of a woman and see how these traits fit with the role of the wife.

> **In like manner, you married women, be submissive to your own husbands [subordinate yourselves as being secondary to and dependent on them, and adapt yourselves to them], so that even if any do not obey the Word [of God], they may be won over not by discussion but by the [godly] lives of their wives. When they observe the pure and modest way in which you conduct yourselves, together with your reverence [for your husband; you are to feel for him all that reverence includes: to respect, defer to, revere him — to honor, esteem, appreciate, prize, and, in the human sense, to adore him, that is, to admire, praise, be devoted to,**

deeply love, and enjoy your husband]. Let not yours be the [merely] external adorning with [elaborate] interweaving and knotting of the hair, the wearing of jewelry, or changes of clothes; but let it be the inward adorning and beauty of the hidden person of the heart, with the incorruptible and unfading charm of a gentle and peaceful spirit, which [is not anxious or wrought up, but] is very precious in the sight of God.

1 Peter 3:1-4

Notice that the Scripture says "You married women, be submissive to your own husbands." It doesn't say here or anywhere else in the Scripture women are to be submissive or subservient to "men." It doesn't say women are second or beneath "men" in any way. It speaks only of the marriage relationship because there must be one giver and one receiver.

As wives we are to willingly put ourselves under — as being secondary to and dependent on — our husbands. It doesn't say you *are* dependent. It says "willingly choose" to *be* dependent. Not because you are, but because he needs you to be. Do you see the difference? You may be the most independent personality on earth, but try to get a seed without him. As a receiver of life, you are dependent on him.

A MASK OF PRIDE

I have always been independent and self-sufficient. I believe the abuse I experienced in my childhood caused me to put up walls. Unconsciously, I would not allow myself to be dependent on any man. This carried over into my marriage.

I spoke earlier about the lack of willingness in my obedience to Harry. I know this was a stumbling block for me. When I kept saying, "I know this isn't all my husband's fault," this was where I was wrong.

On the outside I was adorning myself with all the trappings of a submissive, beautiful wife, but on the inside my heart was corroded and ugly. I was not showing Harry the honor and respect due him. My spirit was not peaceful and gentle. It was anxious and wrought up. That's why Harry wasn't won over by my "discussions" — begging, pleading and crying for him to take his rightful place as spiritual leader. My so-called humility was nothing more than a mask of pride.

So I don't care how independent you are, I don't care how self-confident and self-sufficient you are. I'm saying to willingly be who God has called you to be to your husband. Accept the fact that God has made you the receiver and enjoy your position.

It's a great position. You don't have to come up with anything. You just be the receiver. It's a free gift given to you. You don't have to earn it.

You are the receiver of life. You have the egg, he has the seed. And he plants within you, just like God plants in the Church, and then you get to procreate. It is easy to understand this in natural fertility, but it is the same in the spiritual and soulish realm. We need our husband's "seed" to help us produce our godly character in marriage too.

Notice in 1 Peter, chapter 3, verse 1, it says to be **dependent on them, and adapt yourselves to them.** To be adaptable means to be flexible. God has put within the woman, within the female side of God, an adaptability or flexibility that He has not put within man. It is by this flexibility in your spiritual walk, not by the rigidity of religion, that you will win your husband. This does not mean to compromise your values or God's spiritual laws. It means be adaptable and flexible in any situation. Be a peacemaker and allow God to handle the rest.

> **If possible, as far as it depends on you, live at peace with everyone.**
> **Romans 12:18**

First Peter 3:2 says we must observe the pure and modest way in which we conduct ourselves. This is important because men are visual. They watch what you do more than they hear what you say. This is an important key to communicating with men. They would rather see a picture than hear a picture. That means your body language is more important even than the words that you speak.   ·

Did you know that only 7 percent of good communication involves spoken words, 38 percent is transmitted by voice inflection, and 55 percent by body language and expression? Our eyes are a doorway to our heart — our spiritual eyes as well as our physical eyes.

A GIVER AND A RECEIVER
ᑫᓅ

Let me make one point clear. Being a giver and a receiver is not just about having babies. It has a spiritual dimension as well. As you allow your husband to give into your life, you will receive the freedom and fulfillment to be all you are meant to be as a wife and as a woman of God.

You may be thinking, *Well, what is the husband supposed to do in this scenario?* We have already read in Ephesians 5 that husbands are to **love their wives as [being in a sense] their own bodies** including nourishing, carefully protecting and cherishing them. Now let's look at what it says in 1 Peter 3:7.

> **In the same way you married men should live considerately with [your wives], with an intelligent recognition [of the marriage relation], honoring the woman as [physically] the weaker, but [realizing that you] are joint heirs of the grace (God's unmerited favor) of life, in order that your prayers may not be hindered and cut off. [Otherwise you cannot pray effectively.]**

As women we've thought to ourselves and sometimes said with our mouths, "My husband never tells me I'm pretty. I just want to be adored." If you look closely, it does not say anything in the Word about husbands adoring their wives. It says they are to nourish protect and cherish, but it doesn't mention adore.

It says repeatedly wives are to adore their husbands. That may seem to be the opposite of what we've been taught or the way we think, but when you adore him, it feeds a need all men have to be noticed and admired and reverenced. That may sound like prideful ego, but it is a very real and natural need for a man. It's part of who he is — a God thing in him — the male side of God in him. Just try putting this into action and see how your husband responds.

THE POWER OF AGREEMENT

Take some time to study these Scriptures in more depth and latch onto the concept that God is both male and female.

He's all of us, and you can't have one without the other. That's why the power of agreement is so important. When a husband and a wife unite and get in agreement, they are the most like God they can become. Isn't that awesome?!

That is how the Church is meant to function as well — in that kind of agreement and unity. God never called us to be "lone rangers." That is why marriages are failing, and the Church is not successful in reaching the world for Christ. We are called to be part of a team — the body of Christ.

Now that I finally understand the power of agreement and the unity in which God wants me to walk as a wife and as His servant, I can truly *be #1 at being #2.*

Now that I understand that it isn't how I look on the outside but how my heart looks on the inside, I can relax and enjoy Harry's leadership, love and protection.

We have a long way to go and much more to learn, but Harry and I have determined in our hearts to destroy that two-headed monster. Harry has stepped into his rightful place as the head of our home, and our hearts are joined as one.

CHAPTER 6

Respecting Authority

HARRY SALEM II

"God, I want to do it Your way." I spoke those words to the Lord in 1980 in a Kenneth Hagin crusade as I drew a mark in the sand, rededicating myself to God and His will for my life. From that point I began walking down a long road of submission to authority and rank above me. I began to actively "feel" called to be #2, called to make someone else look good, sound good, be successful. Such a call has to be from God because human nature tells us to "raise ourselves up." Only a godly, spiritual nature leads us to "lift someone else up."

As Cheryl shared in the last chapter, God has a divine order of authority which we cannot escape. In worldly terms this is called a chain of command. It applies to our homes, our ministry and our work. There can be only one head in any of these three areas of life.

A HEAD MUST HAVE A BODY

It is also a fact that a head must have a body. One can't function without the other. Such an order is vital for balance and success. Jesus is the head of the Church, but we, the Church, are His body. Without us, His purposes will not be fulfilled on this earth. Without Him, we can't do what He has called us to do.

At some point in time, everyone is called to function in a support role or #2 position. Jesus *chose* to be #2 when He came to walk upon the earth as a man in order to fulfill the will of the Father. When we find ourselves in the position of being #2, we also have a choice to make — be committed to that #2 position and give it our very best *or* try to compete with the person who is #1.

COMMITMENT, NOT COMPETITION
✂

Cheryl and I take our commitment very seriously. If we were in competition every time we stepped up to the pulpit, we would be striving against each other instead of complementing each other's giftings and strengths. If we compete against each other at home, our home will be filled with strife and discontentment. Our children most likely will react in fear and rebellion to this division and lack of order. The same would apply if I tried to compete with President Roberts at the University.

Submission to the proper chain of command in each situation is critical because competition puts you where you shouldn't be, perpetuating failure. Commitment puts you where you are supposed to be, contributing to success. Whatever you do as #2, do it with the desire to make the #1 person look great, not with a desire to show up whoever is #1.

I remember witnessing this example of someone who wanted to compete rather than commit. I was in California with a group of men who also were traveling with their superiors in a support role. Our bosses had been in a lengthy meeting which had just finished. However, no one had come out of the meeting room yet.

One fellow was pacing the floor anxiously looking at his watch. I asked him what was wrong and couldn't believe his reply. He said, "My boss always takes his sweet time and never thinks of anyone else's schedule. I'm going in and pull him out of there. The meeting is over, and he's not doing anything important anyway. I have an appointment, and he isn't going to make me late again!"

I convinced him that he shouldn't interrupt because he wasn't invited, and he wasn't going to interrupt my boss. I added that we were there to accommodate our bosses, not for them to accommodate us. He arrogantly replied, "I'm not playing second fiddle to anyone. If you want to be someone's 'yes boy,' go ahead; but I'm not going to be anyone's 'doormat.'" What an attitude! I found out shortly thereafter that he and his boss had parted ways.

SUBMISSIVE, NOT SUBSERVIENT
❧

The destructive mentality that says, if you work for someone in a secondary role that means you are subservient, can only be eliminated by you and how you handle your position. It is your choice whether you react defensively or respond gracefully to situations in which you are challenged by the negative attitudes or actions of others.

Being submissive to someone in authority over you is different than being subservient to them. In *The Synonym Finder* by J. I. Rodale, synonyms for the word "submissive" are yielding, compliant, agreeable, adaptable, obedient, faithful, obliging, respectful. Synonyms for the word "subservient" are servile, ingratiating, bowing, scraping, fawning, cowering, self-effacing, bootlicking.[1]

You can easily see the positive characteristics of being submissive versus the negative characteristics of being subservient. When Jesus said we were to submit to those in authority over us, He meant we were to show them respect, not crawl on our knees and lick their boots. There is a big difference.

One day a man called President Robert's office at the University. He was out of town so the call was directed to me. After a brief introduction, the man rudely responded by telling me he did not want to talk to some "subordinate." I explained my position to him and said I would be glad to help him in any way I could. He would not have anything to do with me and repeated his opinion of me as a "subordinate" — a subservient to say the least in this man's mind.

I have never seen myself as subservient to President Roberts, and he has never treated me in that way. I have been treated as a fellow worker, a co-laborer and an important person in my area of work.

This mutual respect is important. When your superior values what you do, this appreciation motivates you to go out of your way to please him or her. It isn't a competition but a commitment to do your best, and as a result you are rewarded accordingly.

The understanding and application of these concepts regarding commitment and submission are critical at home as well as in the workplace. Cheryl and I are totally committed to each other and to living in godly order in our home. We are one in spirit and flesh. We respect each other's position. Our children understand the "chain of command." I am the head of the home and Cheryl submits to me — she is NOT subservient. We are co-laborers together.

A UNITED FRONT

The children know when daddy isn't home, mommy is in command. We support each other and stand as a united front. If Cheryl makes a decision or disciplines the children while I am at work, she usually calls and lets me know what has happened. Then when I get home, I support her in that action.

If Cheryl and I disagree about a decision, we never contradict each other in front of the children. We go aside and discuss the problem privately and make a decision together. If it results in a change in some decision or action that affects the children, we sit down with them and explain the change and why the change was made. This establishes the chain of command and authority in the home. The children understand it, and it gives them a sense of security. It also provides an example for them to follow in later years in their own homes.

This same principle of maintaining a united front and disagreeing in private is equally important in the workplace. No two people think the same way, and it is inevitable there will be disagreements. There is nothing wrong with stating your opinion or expressing your feelings. Just be sure it is done respectfully and in private.

It's like what happens in a jury room. There can be all kinds of confrontation and questioning in the jury room, but when the jury comes back into the court with their verdict, they must be in one accord.

Ask the Lord to show you the right time to approach your superior and to give you the right words to speak. Gather important facts and documentation on the subject, and then set up a meeting to discuss it. Be sure to remember ultimately it is his or her decision *and* responsibility, not yours. Even if you never come to an agreement on the issue, you will know in your heart you expressed yourself in a respectful manner.

Let your boss know you will support whatever decision is made, and thank him or her for hearing you out. When you leave the meeting, keep your opinions to yourself in public and stand by your word. And never, never say, "I told you so," if you turn out to be right.

TOUGH DECISIONS, TOUGH ACTION

When you are not the one calling the shots, tough decisions made by top management may require you to take tough action and implement plans to support those decisions. It is painful when those decisions and actions affect the lives of other people, but you do what you have to do out of obedience and respect for those in authority.

Over the years both the Ministry and the University have had to tighten their budgets. My heart hurt when I had to cut the University operating budgets and expect the managers to manage departments with less money and fewer staff members. At that time I was still hiding my emotions, and many of the staff didn't think I cared what was happening to their people.

68

I recall one time after spending countless hours with managers trying to accomplish this budget-cutting task, I was so stressed I ended up flat on my back in bed for ten days with an inflamed sciatic nerve. I displayed little emotion but inside it was killing me.

A few years later I was faced with a similar situation concerning the television staff. This time I dealt with it differently. I did what had to be done, but I didn't hide my emotions. It helped all of us and was much less stressful. I hurt for them, and I hurt with them. We all hurt together, but we knew we would all live to see a better day — and we have!

When you are in a #2 position, it is sometimes difficult to know when and how to express your opinions. You may even question the value of what you can bring to the table. The worst thing you can do is to think you are the most intelligent person in the room. If you do, you will eventually find yourself alone in that room. So how do you know when to speak up and when to shut up? It's just that black and white!

SPEAK UP OR SHUT UP?
❧

I learned a valuable lesson when I was only twenty-three years old. I was privileged to attend a meeting with fifty other administrators. A million dollar project proposal was being presented by a consultant, and I thought to myself, *don't get involved, just observe. These people must know more than me concerning this project, so I'll just sit here and be quiet — listen and learn.*

God must have had other plans that day. Have you ever been in a situation like that? You are trying to learn and grow by observation, and you begin to get drawn into the scene by an unseen force! The discussion of this project began to take a turn in the direction of the areas of my responsibility. I remember looking around and seeing people glance over at me for my response. At this juncture I could only base my response on my opinion, no real facts, just my gut instincts.

The project involved a massive satellite teleconferencing of meetings all over America. It was a huge spectrum! I was scheduled to be in Africa at that time and was not involved in the project. I felt it was best just to keep quiet and keep peace instead of voicing my concerns.

Then someone in the room said, "What does Harry have to say about this?" I was stuck. I had no other alternative but to give some input. True to my character, I told exactly how I really felt, my concerns, the problems I saw, etc.

The next thing I knew I was asking point blank questions I hadn't even realized were stuck in the back of my mind. I was on a roll and not a supportive one at that. I felt Dr. Winslow, the CEO of the City of Faith at that time, nudge me, and I thought he was implying it was time for me to shut up. So I did and sat down.

The consultant tore into me like a rabid dog defending his project. He began a personal attack on me like I had never before experienced. I was pretty upset and was telling myself I should have kept my opinion to myself! But I knew deep down what I said had value and needed to be voiced. I looked at Dr. Winslow, and he was smiling. I whispered to him, "Now, I know I should have just shut up. I'm too young, and I was out of order voicing my concerns."

Dr. Winslow leaned over and said to me quietly, "No, you were right in what you said and even how you said it.

Most importantly, why you said it has now surfaced. You obviously care for this ministry and desire to protect it. You have exposed those who don't. The problem was when you spoke, whether you realized it or not, you were representing the feelings of your superiors here at the ministry, and the consultant knew it. He was threatened, and you got the brunt of his reaction."

OPINIONS AREN'T YOUR OWN

I asked him what I should have done differently. Dr. Winslow responded, "I don't see what you could have done differently, but in the future, remember this. When you hold a position of authority and speak your opinion, you're perceived to be expressing the opinions of those to whom you report. That is something you must deal with and accept. Be cautious never to think that your opinion will be thought of as your own. It will be perceived to be that of others in higher authority above you, and that is an awesome responsibility. Remember, you are here for a purpose. You are trusted. Never do anything to lose or compromise that trust."

I look back at that million dollar project, and I'm glad I spoke up no matter what the personal cost. But I know now I was speaking for my superiors. With that responsibility I need to be cautious with my words, presentation of ideas, and above all my attitude!

You are a representative of those you work for and should at all times fashion yourself accordingly. Whether it is your appearance, grammar, ideas, opinions or actions, it's not you speaking. It is those you are speaking for who said the words, no matter whose mouth it came out of! The public will remember who you work for or represent before they will remember your name.

REFLECTION OF AUTHORITY

Jesus spoke to us in His Word about authority. He respected authority and knew that everything He said and did was a reflection of His Father who had sent Him. He spoke of this in John 14:10 NKJV, **I do not speak on My own authority; but the Father who dwells in Me does the works.** He remained humble and did not take credit away from the Father in whose authority He acted.

Likewise, we are to show respect for God's divine order of authority whether it is in the workplace or at home. As we remain humble in serving others, so then will we be lifted up. Jesus said it in Luke 18:14 NKJV, **For everyone who exalts himself will be humbled, and he who humbles himself will be exalted.** So believe it! Walk it out in your life, and you will be justly rewarded.

Determined in Your Mind and Heart

HARRY SALEM II

After working for over sixteen years with the Oral Roberts Ministry, I have learned many things, but this lesson sticks out in my mind. Oral asked me to consider overseeing the building of the physical plant of a new television station. A few days later he asked, "With all the other things you are doing, have you made up your mind to build this station for me yet?" I said, "I will do whatever you want me to do." His response was, "No, I want you to do it right. You have to determine in your mind that you are going to do this. You must have the right spirit and see it through." Boy, did that stick with me.

The key is not to just make up your mind to do something but to determine in your mind that you are going to complete the task at hand. To successfully accomplish that task, you have to let it become a part of you. You have to let it get inside your being — in your spirit. Then it becomes not something that you have to do, but something you are committed to doing. Determine in your heart with all your being you are going to accomplish great things.

DON'T JUST DO IT!

NIKE's slogan, "Just Do It," has become so popular you hear it being used in many everyday conversations. It sounds simple to say to someone, "just do it," but I don't buy that. If you're given a task to do, you have to be committed to that task. You have to be sold on it in order to give it your all and do it right.

Here's an example of what I'm saying. When I worked on Dr. Roberts' book tour, I booked him on Larry King, Tom Snyder, and other such television programs. I knew the people and I made the contacts, but it was Oral's book that was being sold. I made sure it was done right because I was committed to Oral, who and what he represents, and what the book said.

Not long after that I was in a Dallas meeting when a man came up to me and said, "I know you worked on Oral's book tour. Would you do the same thing for my book?" He gave me a copy of the book.

After I read it, I contacted him and said, "No, I can't work on your book tour, because I don't believe in the book." He said, "What do you mean?" I said, "I don't believe in some of the principles in the book." He said, "Well, you don't have to believe in the book to help me promote it." I said, "Yes, I do. I knew what Oral was about, I knew what his book was about, and I was committed to the promotion. Because I believed in the book, I could help promote it in the very best way I knew how. I cannot be committed to promote your book, because I don't believe in everything that you've written."

If you get a job and you're given a task to do, but you don't believe in what you are doing or you don't believe in the person or organization for whom you are doing it, you cannot be committed to the task and complete it effectively. If you try to push ahead without resolving the conflict within you, you're just going through the motions, because you haven't bought into it.

Your heart's not in it, and before long it shows up in your attitude. You start murmuring about it to your friends and co-workers and before the task is completed, seeds of discord have been sown. Sometimes it spreads up the ranks; and when it gets up the ladder, you get called on the carpet by your boss.

THE BUCK STOPS WITH YOU!

∾

Now I'm not saying you will always agree with everything that happens in the workplace. But when it's a matter of your principles and values, that's when the buck stops with you. Be man enough or woman enough to say to your superior, "I do not agree with what you are doing or what you are asking me to do." Then explain why you don't agree. Be sure you speak respectfully, never in anger, and always do it privately.

In my own experiences, I have stood up to my superiors and to other people by saying, "I cannot do that, because I don't agree with it. You may find somebody else in your organization who will agree with you and do it, but I can't put my name on it." It has always resulted in a favorable resolution being worked out.

It isn't an easy thing to do, but it's necessary to maintain your integrity and character. You can say, "That's a moral dilemma," or you can say, "It's just my judgment, but I've got to look in the mirror in the morning and shave that face looking back at me."

If your boss is not listening to you or doesn't have enough trust in what you say when you share how you feel about something that goes against your principles or values, you may be faced with making a tough decision. Remember, God expects you to live by His principles without compromise, and the buck stops with you. It may mean removing yourself and saving them the paycheck because you're doing no good for them.

When I was vice president of operations at the University, I wanted everybody to like me, but being popular isn't a criteria for being a good manager. Sometimes it means having to make tough decisions that will affect people's lives and their livelihood. Such decisions don't always allow you to be "Mr. Nice Guy," but they're necessary for the future good of the organization.

Sometimes it means doing things in a specific way that the employees can't understand. I always tried to give my staff as much information as possible to explain decisions, but it's not always possible or appropriate to share all of the criteria behind a decision.

Here's a classic example a friend once shared with me. She was the vice president of a healthcare corporation and was overseeing a multi-million dollar building project. There were two different federal funding agencies involved in financing the project. A major design change order amounting to over $500,000 was discovered after the financing had been approved, and both agencies needed to be involved in determining who was going to be responsible for this additional cost.

Since the two federal agencies were in different cities, the cost of airfare to fly several executives to both locations was going to be well over $2,000. In exploring different transportation alternatives, it was discovered a limousine could be rented for only $300 a day. Although it would mean a sixteen-hour day to go by limousine to the first city, the executive team decided to sacrifice their time and save the costly airfare.

When the limousine arrived at the hospital at 6:30 a.m. to pick up the executives, the night and day shifts were just changing. What a terrible stir there was among the hospital staff that day as everyone was gossiping about the executives "throwing away the hospital's money on limousines." The hospital staff didn't know how much money had been saved by renting the limousine. They made a judgment without knowing all the facts.

JUST LIKE MEDICAL TRIAGE

❧

Whoever is making the decisions has to decide who needs to get the information and whether it will benefit the situation. There are some people who just cannot handle all of the information. So you can't tell them everything, because they wouldn't understand it anyway.

I think management in a crisis situation is like medical triage in a disaster. A doctor has to look at each of the injured and make a quick assessment of who can be saved with the resources available and who is too far gone. Management decisions also have to often be made in the order of importance determined by the resources available and with the understanding there are going to be some casualties. Information is given out to the press or the public only as time and circumstances allow.

It's like cancer, you take off the fingers to save the arm. It's not your first choice, but it happens. And the people who are the fingers just don't understand why they got cut. They didn't do anything wrong. Maybe they just came and worked in this area because at one time that was the priority of need but the need no longer exists.

I've had to shut down a complete department — the whole staff — in one day. They were asking, "What did we do wrong?" And I had to say, "You haven't done anything wrong, but circumstances have dealt this."

When my father was in the automobile industry in Michigan, assembly line workers would get laid off and say, "I came every day. I worked every day and gave everything I had, how come me?" It's like the military draft lottery. I was born on such and such date, how come mine came up 001? I don't know. I have no idea. There are a lot of things that just aren't fair.

DON'T BE TRANSPARENT!
❧

Whether you're #2 in a ministry, in a business organization, or in your home, here is one trap to avoid. Don't be transparent. What I mean is, don't pass the buck to the person above you if an unpopular decision has been made. There is nothing more destructive to a home when the children are unhappy about a decision their dad has made if the mother says, "Well, it's not my fault, go talk to your father."

The same is true in an organization. If top management has made a tough decision and staff members are upset, you will undermine your own management effectiveness if you pass the blame off onto your superiors. A husband and wife need to stand as a united front and so does a manager with his or her superior. If you want to *be #1 at being #2,* you must accept that the buck stops with you. Being transparent not only undermines the person who is #1, but it destroys your own effectiveness as #2.

THE VIEW IS ALWAYS THE SAME
⚬⚬

One of my favorite sayings is, "If you're not the lead dog, the view is always the same." What that means to me is, if you are called to be #2, then you must determine in your heart to die to self and be comfortable in your role. You've got to be happy and love it. Grow where you are planted; blossom where you are.

There are advantages to not being the lead dog. Becoming the lead dog means when you are running, the wind is coming at your face and you're fighting all the battles head on. If you're #2, you're always girded and somewhat sheltered from the wind because ultimate responsibility rests with #1. Your ability to truly *be #1 at being #2* requires that you have it determined in your mind where you are called to be, and it requires a high level of maturity.

Scotty Pippin of the Chicago Bulls is a prime example of *being #1 at being #2.* When Michael Jordan retired, there was a lot of pressure on Pippin; and he tried to step into that #1 role, but everybody said, "He's no Michael Jordan. He will never be Michael Jordan."

When Jordan came back, Pippin stepped back into his #2 role for the sake of the team and look at the success they have had. He is a great complement to Jordan, and together they have reaped great rewards — five championships. Pippin recognizes where he can be the best and accepts he will never be a Michael Jordan. He's not competing, he's supporting, and together they are winning.

In his book, *The Top Ten Mistakes Leaders Make,* Hans Finzel shares this wonderful legend about the importance of humbly serving as part of a winning team. "As construction began on a magnificent cathedral, an angel came and promised a large reward to the person who made the most important contribution to the finished sanctuary.

"As the building went up, people speculated about who would win the prize. The architect? The contractor? The woodcutter? The artisans skilled in gold, iron, brass, and glass? Perhaps the carpenter assigned to the detailed grillwork near the altar? Because each workman did his best, the complete church was a masterpiece.

"When the moment came to announce the winner of the reward, everyone was surprised. It was given to an old, poorly dressed peasant woman. What had she done? Every day she had faithfully carried hay to the ox that had pulled the marble for the stonecutter."[1]

Determine in your mind to accomplish what is in your heart whether it involves your ministry, your family or your business. Don't let pressure from others influence you or change your direction. Only be directed, changed or molded by God. He leads correctly and properly for your ultimate future. The effort you put forth will be far less than the benefits you reap as it says in Luke 6:38 NKJV: **Give, and it will be given to you: good measure, pressed down, shaken together, and running over will be put into your bosom. For with the same measure that you use, it will be measured back to you.**

Determine in your heart of hearts that you **can do all things through Christ who strengthens** you (Philippians 4:13 NKJV). You can succeed in anything that God has ordained for you and complete any dream He has placed in your heart.

Visions of the Heart

CHERYL SALEM

I've spent my life dreaming. Every step of my life has been built on a dream. Everything I've ever accomplished from walking again after my accident, to playing piano and singing, to leaving the country and going to college, to becoming Miss America was a goal, a dream, a vision. I can't imagine not having a dream or a vision to be believing for and reaching toward.

A LONE RANGER

I always was kind of a lone ranger. I did my own thing and followed my own dream. Then I moved to Tulsa and became a part of Oral and Richard Roberts' Ministries. I found out I could accomplish a lot more when I attached my dreams to their dreams and allowed my dreams to flourish because of supporting and helping them accomplish theirs. By planting seed into somebody else's dream, then your dreams will succeed. My seeds were my time, money, ideas and talents. I had to sow into their dream before I could reap and accomplish my own.

For instance, I had always wanted to do women's conferences. Lindsay Roberts and I became fast friends when I came to Tulsa, and she shared her desire to have a women's conference. We teamed up and together were able to accomplish more than either of us could have done singly.

Lindsay had the avenues and resources through the University and Richard's ministry and television show to promote and provide the physical facilities for a large conference. I had the dream and the "let's do it" motivational gift. Together we created a great women's conference which has grown year by year.

Yes, the conference has Lindsay's name on it, but the point is not whose name is on it because it is for God's glory not ours. I get to sing and speak and teach at every conference, and I don't have to worry about any of the detailed logistics of the conference. I've had the joy of seeing women's lives changed and transformed.

When Harry and I were first married I would say, "Share your dreams, your visions with me." And he would say, "I don't have any!" I just could not comprehend that, and I would get upset thinking he just didn't want to share with me. So, for years I went out and followed my vision for ministry.

Harry didn't take part in my vision even from an emotional standpoint, and we walked separately because of it. I was going one way and he was going another. We were like friends talking about what we did, but we weren't involved in each other's roles.

I thought I had to go out and preach and sacrifice my husband, my children, my health and everything to do what

God had called me to do. When I finally got a revelation from God's Word in 1 Peter 3 and Ephesians 5, which I talked about in Chapter 5, I realized God never asked me to do that. It is not His way to destroy a home to bring about ministry.

Then I got a clearer picture and understanding that God's vision was for our home, our marriage and our children to be prosperous and out of that He would bring about the vision of my heart for ministry. It was not Cheryl's ministry, but it was the Salem Family Ministry God wanted to create. He has brought it about three-fold through Li'l Harry, Roman, and Gabrielle; and it can multiply from there.

A SEASON FOR EVERY VISION

Now I see it and wonder why I didn't see it eleven years ago, but I didn't. We have to realize there is a season for every vision of the heart. Elisha had a great call on his heart. He realized he could accomplish his vision more quickly by getting Elijah's mantle than trying to do it himself. So he followed Elijah around, and he got a double portion because of catching Elijah's mantle and anointing. He wound up with twice as many miracles in his ministry. Of course, he wound up with twice as many battles as well. Everything in Elisha's life was doubled — persecution, trouble and miracles. This is a good spiritual example of attaching yourself to someone else's vision.

The disciples all laid down their work, their careers, their families, their visions and dreams to follow Jesus. I didn't realize when I married Harry that ultimately God was calling me to lay aside what "I" wanted to do in life in order to accomplish what He wanted to do with my life. Then I found out what He wanted to do was even better than what my vision had been. Now Harry and I have the same vision and the same hope and the same desire, but we went down a hard, rocky road to get where we are today.

When Harry would tell me he didn't have any dreams, I could not comprehend what he was saying. You see, all my life I had been able to live out my dreams, but Harry's life had been very different. When he was a little boy, he dreamed of having a father-son relationship, but his father died. Then he wanted to play professional baseball, but he got hurt. He wanted to become a pilot, but his poor vision destroyed that dream.

Every dream or desire he had was somehow blocked, and that's when he discovered he could attach himself to someone else's dream. He met two men who had a dream — Oral and Richard Roberts — and he plugged into and became a part of their dream. By helping to bring their dream to fruition, he was fulfilled.

It is important for a couple to discover and share their hopes and desires and dreams before they get married. Because if you are a dream- and vision-oriented person and you marry someone who isn't, you're going to be frustrated.

If Harry and I had been able to communicate better earlier in our marriage, we could have eliminated a lot of the difficulties we faced. Many people would have given up and quit. Of course, God never wants us to quit, but if we could have gotten into unison under the same oxen yoke, we would have had a smoother road to walk.

I was so dream-oriented I would not give Harry any peace. I would say, "Oh, surely you have a dream. Oh, come on now, let's talk about this." I would try to manufacture a dream for Harry. I just couldn't let it go. Now I look back and realize I should have just whet his appetite and let God take over. But I kept pushing him until he would get upset and rightfully so.

A DREAM OR A CALLING?

❧

When Harry was saying he didn't have a dream, it wasn't that he didn't desire one. What I called a dream, Harry couldn't relate to because in his life no dream had been attainable. But Harry did believe you could have a calling — something that you want to do more than anything else in the world. Do you see how we were talking about the same thing but using different words? Is it any wonder we struggled for so long over this issue?

It took God to finally get us talking the same language and to implant His vision into us. Harry's deepest desire was to have a family. For a time and season he was called to attach himself to someone else's dream, but recently the Lord has released him from that role. My dream has always been to minister the Word of God to others and see lives changed.

Now we share the same vision to minister together as a family. We are traveling together living out Harry's dream of having a family and my dream of ministering the Gospel. Harry is catching onto his own vision for leading this family ministry and recognizes the anointing God has on his life. He's more and more comfortable in the pulpit and shares the Lord's wisdom with wonderful practical application. God has truly joined the visions of our hearts.

Your Piece of the Puzzle

HARRY SALEM II

The key to *being #1 at being #2* is not who you are or where you are, it's what you are on the inside. You have your own character makeup. You have your own personality, and you are your own person. What you are on the inside is your character, what you are made of, the substance that you are. No one can take that away from you.

When you are doing what you feel led to do and doing it to the very best of your ability, then you are #1. You are an original, and no one else can do what you do exactly like you do it. No one can be your piece of the puzzle!

AN ORIGINAL CLASSIC

If you put a replacement part on your automobile, it's no longer an original. That is why classic cars are more valuable if they have all the original parts. If you remove a piece from a puzzle and put in a replacement piece, does it fit exactly? Are the colors an exact match? Probably not because it didn't come from the original dye lot. So you can be replaced and someone can do your job, but not the way you did it. If you've done your job with excellence, you will be missed because you're uniquely different.

If my top director for a television show gets sick and has to be replaced for a period of time, I can put another person into the director's chair, but the personality and the spirit that he brings with him will give the show a different flavor. The rest of the crew will have to adjust and learn how to respond to his directing. If you are in a position and you're doing everything that you believe the Lord has called you to do, you are uniquely valuable in that position.

Know who you are on the inside and recognize what an important role your piece of the puzzle plays. The puzzle is always incomplete without your piece. If the maintenance crew member at the airport doesn't put fuel in the plane and the pilot can't take off, who is more important, the pilot or the maintenance crew member?

Think about an astronaut who is strapped into the pilot's seat of a space shuttle and trained to fly it. The astronaut has all the knowledge concerning the mission, but without the support staff at NASA, it would be impossible to accomplish the mission. The astronaut gets all the praise and press coverage when the mission is completed. No one knows who was calling the shots at NASA Control Center, but the astronaut knows and so does the #2 person at NASA.

So many times we get our eyes on the most visible player or piece of the puzzle and think he or she is more important. When the plane gets delayed, we want to go up and tell the pilot off or the poor gate attendant, but it's really the guy down there on the ground who didn't prepare the plane who was at fault. So who is more important? Every piece of the puzzle has an effect on all the other pieces.

Here's another way to look at it. You have four fingers and a thumb on your hand. If you cut off your thumb, how difficult will it be to write or pick up something with only those four fingers? If you lose the little toe on your foot, what happens? You have to relearn how to walk. That thumb and that toe each serves a specific, very important function.

Do You Know Who You Are?

To understand the value of your piece of the puzzle you must know who you are. Are you Bob, Bill, Judy, Sam, Susan? Are you someone's wife or someone's husband?

I have been introduced as Cheryl's husband, Miss America's husband, Richard Roberts' brother-in-law, Lindsay Roberts' brother, Oral's son's brother-in-law, vice president of ORU and the television producer. At my children's school, I am referred to as Harry's dad or Roman's dad. I am all of these people rolled into one. All of these names describe me. I have many integral parts that make up the "whole" me. But, most of all, I am who I think I am. Proverbs 23:7 NKJV says, **For as he thinks in his heart, so is he.** Whatever I think of myself is what I become.

I am a blood-bought child of God. I am an original. I am special. I am someone of great value. I am called of God on this earth with a purpose. A great price has been paid for me. I am a vessel of the Lord. I am a man destined to do great things for God. Yes, I have a name, but more importantly, I have a purpose.

For thirteen years I have had a partner with the same purpose as mine because we are a team. We are a team of two who are one in the flesh. Now, when I wake up every morning and look in the mirror, I ask myself what Cheryl and I are going to accomplish this day.

The face in the mirror might not look like much, or the body with it might not feel like much, but I know, in my spirit, I will accomplish something great this day because of who I am IN CHRIST!

Even if my "something great" is just a special word for my children, that will be enough. Or maybe it will be to show compassion on someone who is hurting, like the security guard at ORU whom God sent across my path one day several years ago.

This young man usually had a big smile on his face, but that day he looked down and out, so I asked him what was wrong. He began to tell me his wife had just miscarried a baby. I invited him to come to my office so we could talk.

This took place not long after Cheryl and I had lost Malachi Charles. I said to this young man, "Cheryl and I just had a miscarriage, too. Yes, both of us had a miscarriage. She physically lost the fetus, but *we* lost the child. You see, many times people tend to console the mother and leave the father out in the cold to deal with his grief. Believe me, we have to deal with it, too."

This young man began to tell me his story, his hurt and his despair over the loss. He was even more concerned about how he was to handle his wife's grief. I asked how "he" was feeling and handling the situation.

Puzzled, he asked me what I meant. I pointed out that it was his child too; he had also lost a baby. He said that in his concern for her, he really hadn't thought of what he was feeling.

I told him how I had been through the same ordeal. Not long after Cheryl seemed to have worked through the initial emotions of the loss, I got mad. I was so angry. I felt the pain. I felt awful, and I couldn't tell anyone my feelings.

As this young man began to share his hurt and loss with me, I was able to relate to his feelings, his hurt, his pain, and help him grieve in a healthy way. I told him how God used our seven-year-old son to help me through my hurt.

When I explained the miscarriage to Li'l Harry, he asked me what we had named the baby we lost. He said, "We need to name him so when we get to heaven, we can call him by name." God knew I wouldn't go out and tell someone outside of our family that I was hurting. In talking with my seven-year-old son, I was able to cry with him and share our grief for the loss of my son and his little brother.

As we ended our talk, this young man told me he never thought I had the time to spend with someone like him. He knew I was always on the run and so busy. I said to him, "I saw in your face what I had seen in my own mirror not too long ago. I recognized the pain, and it stopped me in my tracks."

God knew we were going to cross paths that morning, and He made sure I was in the right place at the right time to reach out to this young man to help him express his hurt and pain. God was changing my heart and giving me a depth of compassion for other men who are hurting. I began to get a glimpse of who I was IN CHRIST and how I could impact their lives. My piece of the puzzle was changing and becoming more valuable as God was transforming me on the inside.

In today's corporate climate of downsizing and work-force reductions, it often appears that top management has lost sight of the *vital* roles "people" play in the success of their organizations. They look at positions and not the people who fill the positions. Are they forgetting it takes "people" in positions to perform necessary functions?

People are not parts on a car. They are each a piece of a puzzle which is made up of a multiple number of different sizes, shapes and colored pieces that fit together to form a complete picture — the life of an organization or a family. They are human beings with unique gifts and talents that should be celebrated.

ENOUGH OF JESUS FOR A LIFETIME!
∾

Cheryl is a prime example as Miss America 1980. Over 75 women have filled the role of Miss America. Every year they replace Miss America. But they have *never* replaced Cheryl. Because for that one year, that title or crown per-sonified Cheryl and all that she was on the inside as well as on the outside. Cheryl did not take on the Miss America traits or lose her identity. Cheryl knew who she was IN CHRIST, and she left her mark.

When her reign ended, the one thing they said to her was, "We've had enough of Jesus for a lifetime." So she im-pacted that system and initiated some changes that made it better for those ladies who followed her. She proved you can be a servant of God and win people to the Lord in any walk of life, in anything that you do.

GOD DIDN'T MAKE COOKIE CUTTERS!

Anyone who has raised children will agree unanimously that no two children are alike, even twins. Each one's special and individual personality challenges parents to find out what motivates that child to do or not to do certain things. Discipline and rewards must be applied differently.

A friend who has a set of identical, ten-year-old twin girls once shared how frustrated she becomes on Sunday morning trying to get the family ready for church. One twin is carefree and will put on whatever catches her eye first, whether or not it all matches doesn't matter to her. The other twin will sit on the floor in the closet with ten outfits lying around her and cry because she can't find anything to wear. She has to find just the right outfit for that morning.

At our house we experience these differences all the time. Li'l Harry is a take charge sort of fellow. He loves to sing and minister. He would take over the pulpit if we let him. Roman is quieter and more reserved. It has taken more courage for him to get up and sing in front of the crowds. Roman needs to be encouraged and recognized for his accomplishments. Gabrielle is our little lady but at times she is quite a clown. There is no question she holds her own with the boys.

We thank God for each of our children. Each one is a valuable puzzle piece in our family picture. There would be a gaping hole without any one of them.

FILL YOUR SHOES TO THE TIPTOES!

~

There's an old saying I tell our children, "You fill out the shoes you are wearing to the tiptoes. Don't try to fill someone else's shoes." I had to remind Cheryl of this one day regarding Harry's report card.

Cheryl thought that he should get A's, and she was pushing him so hard he was struggling in school. I pointed out to Cheryl that he's part my son, too, and I didn't get all A's in school. What is important is that he does his best and fills out the test papers with what he knows. Li'l Harry doesn't have to fill Cheryl's shoes or mine. He just has to fill his own to the tiptoes, and we will always be proud of him.

It is impossible for one person to fill another person's shoes. Look at Michael Jordan. How can his son ever fill his shoes? He can't. How can Gabrielle ever fill Cheryl's shoes as Miss America? She can't. How can Chelsea Clinton ever fill her father's shoes as President?

Think about it. God didn't make people from cookie cutters. He made each one of us from a different set of cells. No two cells are identical. How boring life would be if we were all alike. I hate to think what the world would be like with ten Harry Salem II's around! Who knows with cloning maybe it could happen, but I don't believe that is God's desire or plan. I shudder to think where it could lead.

The point I want to make is that whether it is in the family, in business or in ministry it is important to celebrate the uniqueness of individuals, to encourage them to fill out their own shoes to the tiptoes by being who they are. Do all that you can to help them be all God has called them to be.

MOVING OUT OF THE COMFORT ZONE

Up to this point my greatest accomplishments in life came from being the support person — the #2 person. When I went to work, I was comfortable in my role. It worked for me, and if someone tried to get me out of it, I was like an angry dog. I liked where God had put me. I learned many valuable lessons helping the Roberts' reach their goals and fulfill their dreams. I loved going to work in the morning and meeting all the challenges put before me. It was a tremendous training ground.

Now I realize God was preparing me to step into a higher calling. He wants me to be the leader in our home and in our family ministry. For years I have watched with awe as the Roberts' family, Cheryl and others ministered to large crowds. I thought that if I was to physically share in Cheryl's ministry, I would be perceived as competitive. But that's not so. I had no idea that it would only enhance what she does and add to what I've been called to do.

We all have strengths and weaknesses. I am just as strong as my wife in some areas and stronger in others, as is true of her character as well. Together we are jointly fitted together to make one awesome vessel for the Father's purposes.

I know I must heed the call of the Father to step into my rightful role. I recently resigned all of my positions with the

Roberts' ministries and with the University. I will remain available to them as a consultant for special projects.

Not long before I made this decision, Cheryl was talking with Richard one day and he said to her, "Harry is feeling the pull to full-time ministry, isn't he?" Cheryl said, "Yes, but he doesn't want to disappoint you or Oral." Richard said, "He needs to be obedient to God's call. Of course, it will not be easy to lose Harry — most of all I will miss his wisdom."

When Cheryl shared that conversation with me, it was confirmation that I was hearing correctly from God. Another confirmation came when I realized my desire is to minister with Cheryl and my family.

I have a new passion to go out and make a difference in the lives of other men. I want to tell them they don't have to pick up those secular books by the Donald Trumps and others who are telling men to find their inner beings so they can make all the monetary gains and forget about everyone around them. I have a desire to teach them how they can be a family man *and* a success in business.

DAD'S MY HERO!
∽

There was a letter printed in the newspaper from a little boy who had written to his dad and said, "You don't wear a tie to work every day. You don't do this and you don't do that like Johnny's dad next door. You don't drive a new car, but what you do for me means more to me than anything else. You are my hero."

If more kids today could look at their dads and say, "You are my hero," we wouldn't have the problems with gang violence, kids dying from drug overdoses, and teenage suicides. Families today are out of whack. They need to focus on God so the family unit can be strengthened. Men need to take back their ground and be the husbands and fathers they are called to be.

There is a love and a compassion in me for people that I have never felt before. Most men out there have had their walls up, and they think they have to be these macho men, or yuppie businessmen. They have put up barriers that shut out their wives and their children. They are driven by performance and the desire for all the material things money can buy — large houses with six-figure price tags, a swimming pool, a country club membership, not two but three Lexus cars in the driveway, ski vacations and more than the Jones ever dreamed of having.

The kids are busy with dance lessons, karate classes, soccer games and skating parties but they're lucky if they get five minutes with Dad a week. These men can't understand what happened when their wife suddenly announces she wants a divorce, and another family bites the dust.

Before this happens, I want to tell them it doesn't have to be that way. Being a provider isn't enough — they must be a participant in the family as well. It's not too late to get their children back. All they need to do is get down on their knees and talk with their children face to face, so they won't just be an imposing stranger who comes home to sleep. When they let their children see how much they care, suddenly the children will start communicating and sharing their hearts. They grow up so quickly, and if a relationship isn't established in the early years, the teenage years may be tough to weather.

Children need to know Daddy is not this person who works ten or twelve hours a day and comes home mad all the time. Daddy is their dad, their friend and their hero; because in children's eyes heroes don't fail you, heroes don't lose, heroes don't die, heroes can fix anything.

THE FIVE-MINUTE RULE
~

I heard a speaker share his own special way of spending time with his children. He called it the "five-minute rule." Each day when he came home from work, he made it a point to spend five minutes individually, one on one, with each of his children. He was careful never to scold or bring correction during this special time of sharing. It was to be a private time uninterrupted by television or the telephone. As teenagers got involved in sports and other busy schedules, sometimes they had to schedule their five minutes in the evening, but it was scheduled into each day.

Then before dinner he would sit down with his wife for five or ten minutes of quiet conversation. They would just share what had happened during the day. It was a time to listen to each other, not to try to fix everything or get into controversies.

He said he knew how well this five-minute rule was working when one day he heard his teenage daughter on the phone telling her best friend she didn't want to go to the mall because she was going for a walk with Dad! You see, Dad's piece of the puzzle can't be replaced, and in his children's eyes he is more valuable than he can imagine. There is no greater reward than being your son's or your daughter's hero!

HEEDING THE CALL

At one time, heeding my call would have been a big, scary step for me, but when the time came, it was easier than I thought it would be. God is faithful in His provision. The Salem Family Ministry has been booked almost every weekend for months. What a joy it has been for us to travel as a family and minister His Word. Each member of the family lends his or her special touch to each ministry session. Each piece of our puzzle is now in its rightful place. It is our desire to help others learn how to value their puzzle pieces and how to get them in order.

The Rock of Our Foundation

CHERYL SALEM

How many times have you heard someone say, "That Bobby is just a chip off the old block," or "Sally, you are just like your momma"? Quite a few I'm sure. Family likenesses and character traits are easily recognized, and the meaning behind such statements may be based on positive or negative qualities. But how many times has anyone said to you, "When I look at you, I see Jesus," or "You act just like your Father" (meaning your heavenly Father)? It probably hasn't happened very often, if ever.

Jesus was speaking to His disciples in John 14:7 NKJV and said, **If you had known Me, you would have known My Father also; and from now on you know Him and have seen Him.** Philip did not understand this statement and asked Jesus to show them the Father. Jesus responded.

> **Have I been with you so long, and yet you have not known Me, Philip? He who has seen Me has seen the Father; so how can you say, "Show us the Father"? Do you not believe that I am in the Father,**

**and the Father in Me? The words that I speak to you
I do not speak on My own authority; but the Father
who dwells in Me does the works. Believe Me that I
am in the Father and the Father in Me, or else believe Me for the sake of the works themselves.**

John 14:9-11 NKJV

Jesus did only what His Father did. So, when people
saw Him, they were seeing the Father. Likewise, when we
do what we see our earthly father do, those around us see
our earthly father's characteristics and traits — his character
and nature in us. This applies to mothers as well.

It is the natural order of life for offspring to look like
and imitate the action of their parents. If you don't like what
your children do or say, check your own actions and words.
You may find their actions in you!

We were created in the image of God; and just as God is
three in one — Father, Son and Holy Spirit, we were created
three in one — with a body, a soul and a spirit. It is God's desire
for us to display His character and nature in all that we do.

A BIODEGRADABLE EARTH SUIT
∾ᴏ

Our body is what I heard one preacher refer to as our
"earth suit." It houses our spirit and soul while we live and
breathe here on earth. It is made up of flesh and bone and
requires nourishment and care. It is unique from the other
two parts in that it is biodegradable — it will decay and
return to dust. Our spirit and soul are eternal which means
they will live on forever.

Our soul is made up of our mind, will and emotions. It houses our character and personality. The Father loved us so much that He did not create us to be robots or puppets. He wanted us to have all of His attributes including a free will. It is our free will to choose whether our soul and spirit will live in heaven or hell when our life on this earth is over. Therefore, it is our soul that Satan wars to control, because that is where we make our choices regarding life and death, peace and war, love and hate, good and evil, heaven and hell.

Satan attacks our minds and our emotions to try to control our will because he wants to own our soul. Our soul acts like a cloak around our spirit, and if Satan owns our soul he also owns our spirit. It's like that old song that says, "Don't let the devil ride, because if he does, he will want to drive!"

God wanted a family. He wanted sons and daughters to be His partners. Adam and Eve were created by God in His image and lived in the Garden of Eden. They walked and talked with God and their spirits were one with Him. They were created to have relationship with the Father and to fulfill His purposes on the earth. Before sin entered in, they represented the nature of God Himself and displayed all of His character and attributes. They ruled and had dominion over all of the earth.

THE ULTIMATE PARENT

God is the ultimate parent! He wants His children to look and act like Himself. He looks for traits in us that remind Him of Himself. He rejoices when He can say, "Look how My daughter is speaking to that mountain. She's just like Me! She learned that from Me!"

We don't comprehend the magnitude of what God did when He gave man such authority. God made Himself dependent on man. He allowed Himself to be limited by us and hindered by our free will and choices. Man's authority over the earth was so complete, he could even give it away to another. And that is exactly what Adam and Eve did when they sinned. In their disobedience to God, they gave their authority to Satan.[1]

> **The heavens are the Lord's heavens, but the earth has He given to the children of men.**
>
> **Psalm 115:16**

> **What is man that You are mindful of him, and the son of [earthborn] man that You care for him? Yet You have made him but a little lower than God [or heavenly beings], and You have crowned him with glory and honor. You made him to have dominion over the works of Your hands; You have put all things under his feet.**
>
> **Psalm 8:4-6**

When Adam and Eve sinned, they gave the devil legal rights to their persons and to the earth. They became slaves to sin, and through their seed, they passed their fallen sin nature on to future generations. The intimate relationship Adam and Eve had experienced with the Father was broken and man's mind was taken over by Satan's lies and deception. Death overtook their spirits and fear, guilt and shame entered into their emotions. Immediately they began looking to someone else to blame for the choices they had made. They had taken on the nature of Satan and entered into bondage.

> **Do you not know that to whom you present yourselves slaves to obey, you are that one's slaves whom you obey, whether of sin leading to death, or of obedience leading to righteousness?**
>
> **Romans 6:16 NKJV**

It was God's intent for mankind to forever be the link between God and authority on the earth. Therefore, since man had given away his authority, it was only another human who could take it back. Jesus came to earth as a man to take back the authority over the earth from Satan and give it back to God's sons and daughters. He suffered the agony of the cross bearing all of our sin and shame. He took the penalty of our sins upon Himself and went into the depths of hell for three days to liberate our souls from captivity so that our spirits may be one with Him once again to live and reign with Him for eternity.

> **For as by one man's disobedience many were made sinners, so also by one Man's obedience many will be made righteous.**
>
> **Romans 5:19 NKJV**

> **But when the fullness of the time had come, God sent forth His Son, born of a woman, born under the law, to redeem those who were under the law, that we might receive the adoption as sons. And because you are sons, God has sent forth the Spirit of His Son into your hearts, crying out, "Abba, Father!" Therefore you are no longer a**

slave but a son, and if a son, then an heir of God through Christ.

Galatians 4:4-7 NKJV

Through Christ's death and resurrection, Jesus paid for our sins in full and gave us back our authority over the earth *and* over Satan. Jesus did it as a man thereby canceling any legal claim Satan had over man or the earth.

> **Inasmuch then as the children have partaken of flesh and blood, He Himself likewise shared in the same, that through death He might destroy him who had the power of death, that is, the devil, and release those who through fear of death were all their lifetime subject to bondage. For indeed He does not give aid to angels, but He does give aid to the seed of Abraham. Therefore, in all things He had to be made like His brethren, that He might be a merciful and faithful High Priest in things pertaining to God, to make propitiation for the sins of the people. For in that He Himself has suffered, being tempted, He is able to aid those who are tempted.**
>
> **Hebrews 2:14-18 NKJV**

> **[But] he who commits sin [who practices evil-doing] is of the devil [takes his character from the evil one], for the devil has sinned (violated the divine law) from the beginning. The reason the Son of God was made manifest (visible) was to undo (destroy, loosen, and dissolve) the works the devil [has done].**
>
> **1 John 3:8**

As believers in Christ we have a new nature. We are alive in Him and have been set free from the bondage of sin. Why then do so many Christians live such defeated lives? We have already read that Satan has sinned from the very beginning. He is a liar and a deceiver, and he doesn't give up one inch of ground without a fight.

It's Up to Us

Hosea 4:6 says, **My people are destroyed for lack of knowledge.** Many Christians don't know they are free. As we submit to Jesus, we have His authority, but it is up to us to exercise that authority. We also must understand that such authority only operates in the spiritual realm. When we try to respond to Satan in the realm of the soul — with our minds and emotions — it has no effect, because he operates in the spiritual realm. We must use spiritual weapons — prayer, praise, the Word — to defeat our enemy, the devil.

> **For though we walk (live) in the flesh, we are
> not carrying on our warfare according to the flesh
> and using mere human weapons. For the weapons
> of our warfare are not physical [weapons of flesh
> and blood], but they are mighty before God for the
> overthrow and destruction of strongholds.**
> **2 Corinthians 10:3-4**

Jesus is the "Rock" of our foundation. Without Him we cannot be #1 at anything we try to do. We have choices to make every day as to how we live our lives. Acts 17:28 says **in Him we live, and move, and have our being.** Therefore we are not to take it lightly that we are the offspring of God.

He wants us to reveal His nature and character to others. It is our choice. Will we live in righteousness or in darkness? Will our children learn the ways of God from us or the ways of Satan? Will we live in the freedom of the authority Jesus has made available to us or continue to live defeated by the father of lies — Satan?

Ask yourself, "What do others see when they look at me?" Do they see love, trust, faith, humility, obedience and integrity? Do they see Jesus' light shining from your eyes? If you haven't made a firm commitment to live IN CHRIST, to live in victory and not defeat, I hope you will stop right now and pray this prayer, "Lord Jesus, today I choose to live for You. Come into my heart and reign in my soul. I repent of my sins and for placing my will above Your will. Thank You for dying for my sins and rising again so I might be free from Satan's slavery.

"In the authority of Your name I declare I am the body of Christ, and Satan has no power over me, for I overcome evil with good (1 Corinthians 12:27; Romans 12:21). I will fear no evil, for You are with me, Lord; Your Word and Your Spirit they comfort me (Psalm 23:4). I thank You, Lord, that I am a partaker of Your divine nature and the inheritance of the saints in the light. I believe You have delivered me from the power of darkness and conveyed me into the kingdom of Your love (Colossians 1:12-13).

"Continue to reveal to me through Your Scriptures who I am IN YOU that I may walk in righteousness and be an example of You and Your love. I submit myself completely to You and take back the ground Satan and his evil forces have stolen from me and my family.

"Thank You, Lord, for always leading me in triumph IN YOU and for diffusing the fragrance of Your knowledge in every place through me (2 Corinthians 2:14). I love You, Lord, and will keep Your commandments. I receive Your Spirit of truth: I believe in Your victory over Satan.

"By the authority of Your name, I will stand in faith until I experience victory in all areas of my life. I acknowledge that only IN YOU can I be #1 FOR YOU. Praise and glory be to You forever and ever. Amen."

Now be happy! And since you are choosing to be happy, notify your face and smile! You are #1 in your Father's eyes.

CHAPTER 11

Eternal Values

HARRY SALEM II

When Cheryl used to ask me about my goals, the only goal that came to my mind was to have a family. The driving force of that desire came from my Middle Eastern culture which is centered around family heritage. I believe it also came from having lost my father at such a young age and wanting to be able to have sons and daughters of my own to carry on the heritage left by my father.

My mother's love and influence were also major factors in reinforcing the importance of family. I shared in Chapters 1 and 2 how both of my parents taught me the values which shaped my life — responsibility, accountability, love, honesty, trust in God, respect for family heritage, a "never-give-up" attitude, honor and hard work. I am forever grateful to my parents for the character and integrity they instilled in me. Without their love, strength and courage I would not be the man I am today.

America is in crisis today because of the decline in moral and spiritual values that once were taught at home. With the disintegration of the family structure in our country, we are seeing a decline in moral and spiritual values. As people have become more mobile, extended families have little or no influence on growing children. Grandparents and aunts and uncles now live in different parts of the country. A visit once or twice a year provides little opportunity for close relationships to be formed.

The increase of working mothers, divorce and single-parent homes has even watered down the influence parents have on their children. Day care has replaced stay-at-home moms. Family dinners have become a quick trip to the closest fast-food restaurant or pizza in front of the television. If you took a poll of grade school children and asked how many sit down at a table with their entire family even once a week, I'm afraid the results would be alarming. With this we also see a lack of social graces as children are not taught simple table manners and politeness.

What is the impact of this destruction of the family unit and respect for family heritage? The number and size of gangs have increased as young people search for a sense of belonging. Gang violence is not just something that happens in big city ghettos. It now reaches into the middle class and affluent neighborhoods of smaller cities and towns more frequently than ever before.

The number of violent crimes being committed by children and teenagers has increased at an alarming rate. In Dallas, Texas, a fourteen-year-old boy was recently convicted of murdering a much-loved school teacher during an attempted robbery. He was sentenced to forty years in prison before parole. This was not his first brush with violence or with shooting someone in a robbery. He was very small for his age, and it was hard to believe he could be a killer. But his heart was so hard, he showed no emotion or remorse during the trial.

I could go on and on, but you get the point. I can truly say, "But for the grace of God, I could have been one of those statistics of teenage crime or death." I was born and raised in Flint, Michigan, fifty miles outside of Detroit — one of the top ten cities reporting the highest number of murders annually. From the age of ten I had no father figure in the home. My mother struggled to meet our needs. Our extended family basically deserted us at a time when we needed them most. There was plenty of opportunity for anger and bitterness and self-pity. But I thank God for a father and mother who knew the importance of family heritage and godly values.

Cheryl and I are committed to teaching our children about the importance of their family and spiritual heritage. We want them to know who they are and to respect where their ancestors came from. We share our memories, experiences and special family stories with them over and over. Most importantly, we stress the good things we *did* have, not what we didn't have. Too many times parents are so busy giving their children what they didn't have in material possessions, they forget to give them what they *did have* in love, time, etc. We know that we have an awesome responsibility to reveal God's character to Li'l Harry, Roman and Gabrielle.

THE "I" "ME" SOCIETY

In today's society everything seems to revolve around the "I" word. "I" have to do this. "I" want this. "I" need this.

What about me? Who is looking out for me? What's in it for me (WIIFM)? Cheryl and I call this the "I" "Me" society. Besides everything being instant in today's microwave society, everything is "I" and "Me." The trinity of the world is ME, MYSELF, and I. In this society people give to get, not share to receive.

We pray like this, "God, I want this. I need this. What are You going to do for me today? If I give You my offering, what's in it for me?" It's okay to question God, but we must examine what our motive is behind the question.

We must have a godly value system to live by in this self-centered society. Here is a great article which was published in the *Tulsa World* newspaper. It is titled, "Mother of three shares the ABC's of successful parenting skills." You might not be able to remember this whole alphabet, but it is a good set of standards to teach your children to live by.

"A is for accountability. Hold your children accountable for their behavior.

"B is for boundaries. Set specific limits and make clear the repercussions if those limits are exceeded.

"C is for consistency. Hold to the same principles and practices.

"D is for discipline. Make the punishment fit the crime. Never discipline in anger.

"E is for example. Children are in greater need of models than critics. Set a good example.

"F is for forgiveness. Practice it and teach the importance of forgiving.

"G is for giving. Teach the joy of giving not only with family and friends but with strangers in need.

"H is for sense of humor. Keep your sense of humor. Promote laughter within your children.

"I is for imagination. Be creative and play with your children. Make up stories or songs and read and sing with them.

"J is for justice. Be fair and insist that they be fair also.

"K is for knowing your children's friends and their parents as well as their teachers.

"L is for listening. Listen to your children. It will teach them how to listen to others, and their thoughts will give you insights.

"M is for morals. Be sure your own standard of conduct is sound.

"N is for NO! Use it and mean it.

"O is for outdoors. Provide as much outdoor activity as possible. Teach respect for nature.

"P is for pressure. Reduce the pressure on your children but insist they maintain high standards.

"Q is for questions. Pay close attention to their questions and give simple answers unless they ask for more.

"R is for respect. Show respect, teach respect, and earn respect.

"S is for source of strength. Share your own faith or beliefs with your children. Faith can be their port in the storms of life later.

"T is for togetherness. Have special, designated times to be together as a family. Know when to let go as well.

"U is for uniqueness. Understand the uniqueness of each child and let that child be who he or she is.

"V is for voice. Tone of voice can say more to a child than the words that are spoken.

"W is for words. Keep your word. Promises broken destroy trust.

"X is for examine. Examine constantly and be aware.

"Y is for you. Take care of yourself mentally, physically, and spiritually. A happy parent helps a child to be happy.

"Z is for zowie! Who would have thought they would grow up so quickly."[1]

You can easily modify the wording in this alphabet and apply these same standards outside the home. If you truly want to *be #1 at being #2*, make every effort to model them at home, at work, at church, in the grocery store or wherever you are interacting with people.

THE "I-MINDED" PERSON
᠙ᢁ

Let me point out one place in the Bible that talks about an "I-minded" person. In Isaiah 14:12-14 NKJV, take notice of the repetition of the word "I."

How you are fallen from heaven, O Lucifer, son of the morning! How you are cut down to the ground, you who weakened the nations! For you

**have said in your heart: "I will ascend into heaven,
I will exalt my throne above the stars of God; I will
also sit on the mount of the congregation on the
farthest sides of the north; I will ascend above the
heights of the clouds, I will be like the Most High."**

Whenever you encounter an "I-minded" person, you
will also encounter the subtle spirit of competitive jealousy.
This is what caused the downfall of Satan. He compared
himself to the Almighty God and actually believed that he
could compete with the Sovereignty of the universe. That
was the first "I" "Me" in the Bible when Lucifer placed himself in an equal or even higher position than Almighty God.

In today's society do we see athletes do that? Do we see
politicians do that? Do we see neighbors or parents or
bosses do that? Yes, we do. We see that because of the society in which we live. It is indoctrinated into us. We think,
*I've got to go out and do better for "me." No one else will do it for
"me."* It's the "survival of the fittest" mentality. The world
may call that confidence, but God calls it pride. And pride
is the opposite of what brings us to God. Pride separates us
from Him. Humility brings us to Him, and that should be
our ultimate goal. This message is a great foundation for
anyone of any age, and Cheryl will talk more about it in
Chapter 15.

Everyone knows the 23rd Psalm. Cheryl was meditating
on this psalm, and the Lord gave her a revelation about the
first verse which reads, **The Lord is my shepherd; I shall
not want.** It could be interpreted as "The Lord is my shepherd; so I choose to control my wants!" That says a lot.

119

Cheryl and I often teach about the four "I's" that we think are important in overcoming an "I" "Me" society — integrity, intensity, intimacy and inventory. We're going to discuss the first "I" here and then explore the remaining "I's" in the next three chapters.

"I" IS INTEGRITY

The first "I" is integrity. I love the definition I once heard a speaker share. He said, "Integrity is when the person you see yourself as, is the same person that others see you as, and is the same person that God sees you as." How much clearer can it get? When all three see the same picture, nothing is hidden, and true integrity is revealed. My way of saying this is, "You must be true to the face you see in the mirror every morning!"

As a father, I must have the highest integrity before my children. I must set the example for them, because when I do it, "I" do it for "us," the family. I'm not doing it for me, I'm doing it for the family. I take my name and reputation seriously. My Lebanese name — Salem — means peace as in Jerusalem — city (Jeru) of peace (Salem). I am proud of my name and my heritage, and I want our children to be equally proud.

You need to instill in your children your heritage, not only your spiritual, biblical heritage but your own personal heritage so they will have something of substance when they leave the nest. If your parents haven't taken time to do that, then take your own time. Go back and research and find out about your own heritage and from where your family came.

120

It is important to know your roots so you can pass it on to the next generation and the next and the next.

WHAT'S IN A NAME?

When Cheryl was pregnant with each of our children, I spent nine months searching for just the right name for each of them. Harry Assad Salem III's name means "tiger of peace." Roman Lee Salem means "our strength in peace or strongman of peace," and Gabrielle Christian Salem means "God's Christ-like messenger of peace." We remind our children often of the meaning of their names and encourage them to live out their names.

Proverbs 22:1 NKJV says, **A good name is to be chosen rather than great riches, loving favor rather than silver and gold.** In the book of Ruth, the names of Naomi's sons, Mahlon and Chilion, translate as "sick" and "weakly." It's no wonder they died early in life. What we say over our children and each other is so very important.

If you don't feel like your family name is worth passing on, think about this. You can be the first generation to make it worth something. You may not feel you had anything of value passed on to you, but you can begin in your generation making your name or heritage something that your children will be thankful and proud to have handed to them.

The Bible is full of the importance of names. From the beginning to the end, the names that were given were for a reason. It is interesting to note that the very first person in the Bible that God named before he was born was Ishmael

— the father of the Arabic nations — the other half of the Abrahamic covenant. God often changed people's names when they were stepping into a higher calling — Abram became Abraham, Jacob became Israel, Saul became Paul.

GOD'S MEASURE

So what is God's definition of integrity? In Matthew 5:6 NKJV it says, **Blessed are those who hunger and thirst for righteousness, for they shall be filled.** Righteousness is integrity. The definition of righteousness from *Webster's Dictionary* is morally right or justifiably acting in accordance with divine or moral law.[2] How many people in America today say, "I have integrity"? Then they measure the integrity they have by their own standards. There is only one standard by which you should measure integrity — by divine or moral law from the Word of God.

IT'S ONLY A WHITE LIE!

I love Opie Taylor from the Andy Griffith Show. I remember the show in which Opie was going to trade his bicycle with a friend, and it had a broken chain. His dad said, "Did you tell your friend about the broken chain?" Opie said, "No, Dad. If I do, he won't swap with me." Andy said, "You've got to tell him about it."

On the same show Barney is selling real estate, and Andy is going to swap houses with a neighbor. Andy's furnace doesn't work right, and the neighbor's house has a basement that floods every time it rains. Andy isn't going to tell the neighbor about the furnace, and Opie says, "But Dad, aren't you going to tell them about the furnace?" Andy says, "Oh, it's just a little white lie. Don't worry anything about it."

In the next scene you see Opie with the roller skates for which he had swapped his bike. Andy says, "Did you tell him about the broken chain?" Opie says, "No, Dad, it's just a little white lie like you said." Andy thought for a second and said, "You're right!" Opie taught Andy a lesson. He went and told the neighbor they weren't swapping houses. Children learn more from what we do than what we tell them to do.

If we don't teach our children values, they're going to come up with their own values. We're seeing that happen in this generation with teenagers who have no conscience and no sense of right and wrong. If they see something they want, they just take it. Kids in school get beat up because someone wants their expensive athletic shoes. Drivers have been shot and killed because someone wanted the gold wheel rims off their car or truck.

On a TV talk show recently, the host was interviewing girls who are gang members. All but one of the girls were less than sixteen years old, and two were only thirteen. Initiation into the gang required them to beat or even kill someone. At least three of the girls had, in fact, either stabbed or shot someone, and two had killed someone. One girl blatantly described beating a girl from a rival gang with a steel rod and hearing the girl's bones break. She did not display any remorse at having broken a person's leg with her own hands. It has become what they do to have relationship in the gang.

When the host asked if they would want their younger sisters to join the gang and have to do what they had done, they said, "Yes." One of the thirteen-year-old girls on the show was actually the younger sister of one of the other girls, who was proud to have helped teach her younger sister the ropes.

HOPELESSNESS AND APATHY WERE SCREAMING!
⤸

Their sexual lives were equally void of godly values. Two of the girls had babies already. One girl had gone through two or three abortions. Life had no meaning for them, and most of them said they did not expect to live to be adults. Hopelessness and apathy were screaming from each of these girls. These are children who don't know the meaning of love or compassion. The gangs have developed their own value systems from the violence of the streets. What will the heritage be of the next generation?

Here is a great nugget of truth: If we are living just to have life, L"IF"E is full of "ifs"; but if we are living for Jesus, JES"US" is living for and in "us!"

YOU ARE AN AMER-I-CAN!
⤸

Cheryl loves to remind people that we have a national heritage, and it comes in the name, Amer-I-Can. When we say, "I am an American," we are saying, "I Can." I am an Amer-I-Can. Everything that we put our hand to do should teach us that "we can."

Look at it biblically in Mark 9:23: **And Jesus said, [You say to Me], If You can do anything? [Why,] all things can be (are possible) to him who believes!** So put it in your heart that you are not only an Amer-I-Can, but you serve a God in whom all things are possible to accomplish. When you believe in Him and with Him, all things are possible and "can be." You serve a "can be" God and that makes you a "can be" person. Get that established inside of you, and you will walk like it, look like it, talk like it and act like it is so until it is!

You truly "can be" #1 at whatever you do, if you will live according to God's standards of integrity and believe in His Word. You "can be" a godly example for your children and those around you. You "can" instill eternal values into your children that will assure blessings upon them and a thousand future generations. That's the heritage I want for my children and grandchildren and their grandchildren. Don't you?

> **Know, recognize, and understand therefore that the Lord your God, He is God, the faithful God, Who keeps covenant and steadfast love and mercy with those who love Him and keep His commandments, to a thousand generations.**
>
> **Deuteronomy 7:9**

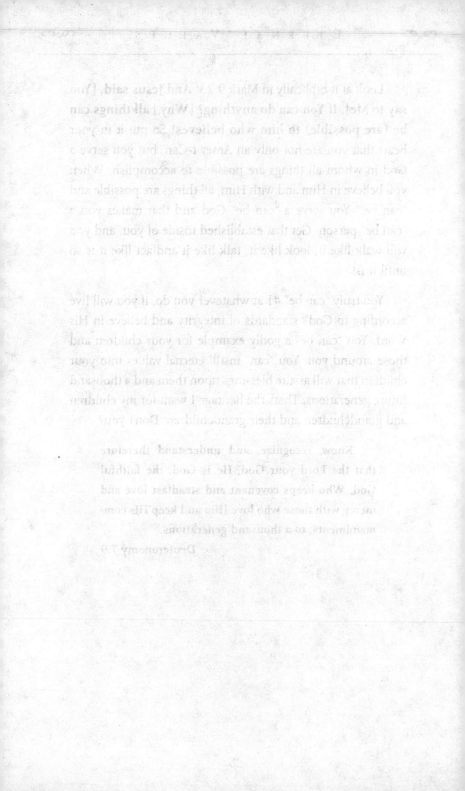

Intimacy Is INTO ME SEE!

HARRY SALEM II

In an "I" "Me" society, intimacy is not a popular subject. The perverted, "self-centered" mentality of this society fears getting too close to someone else. After all, if you can see my weaknesses, then "I" can't maintain control. Lack of intimacy is destroying families and godly relationships every day. It is driving husbands and wives into the arms of others and children into the street gangs. It is even driving people into cults and into the occult. Legitimate needs are being met in illegitimate ways.

Intimacy has been a deeply rooted need in every human being from the beginning of time. God created man in His image because He desired relationship. He walked in the garden daily with Adam, and they had a close intimacy — spirit to Spirit. When Satan deceived Eve and sin entered in, that intimacy was broken. Satan deceived Eve, and he is still deceiving man today into thinking he doesn't need intimacy with God or with man.

The "I" "Me" society says "I" can do it myself, but the truth is we can't. Jesus came to earth as a man. He died and was resurrected to restore man's relationship with the Father. The door to intimacy has been reopened, and we can't do without it. Here's what the Word says.

The Spirit Himself bears witness with our spirit that we are children of God.

Romans 8:16 NKJV

I am the vine, you are the branches. He who abides in Me, and I in him, bears much fruit; for without Me you can do nothing.

John 15:5 NKJV

Intimacy with God in prayer is referred to in 1 Corinthians 6:17 NIV: **But he who unites himself with the Lord is one with Him in spirit.** Cheryl and I are intimate as husband and wife. We are intimate with God, the Father, through our prayers and time alone with Him and in the Word. We have intimate time with our children. We take precious time with our children together and individually in what we call "private time." Intimacy is important for everyone and for every family.

CHILDREN ARE STARVING!
❧

You need to be intimate with God, the Father. You need to be intimate with your spouse and your family. I read an article recently that said most men spend an average of three minutes of quality time a week with their children. That's right, three minutes "a week!" What if they treated their stomachs the way they treat their children? They would starve to death, just as their children are starving for their attention!

If God gives you children and you don't spend time with them, you are letting someone else be intimate with your children. Do you even know who or what they are being intimate with — TV, the internet, ungodly neighbors, school friends, gang members?

Cheryl says intimacy is an easy word to say, but when you break it apart it says, IN TO ME SEE. When I said Cheryl and I are intimate, I'm not talking about it in sexual terms. Intimacy is when we can allow ourselves to be vulnerable.

We need to be vulnerable to the Lord and be able to say, "Lord, I can come before You just as I am. With all the mess and problems in my life, I can allow myself to let the walls down, to throw the covers back, open the doors or do whatever I need to do to be vulnerable to You." Everyday I say to the Lord in my private time, "God, IN TO ME SEE. I don't want to hide anything from You. I don't want to have things I can't tell You." When Cheryl and I have our time together, it's IN TO ME SEE, Cheryl, and IN TO ME SEE, Harry.

If you aren't intimate with your mate and are asking how you can develop that closeness, just think back to when you were dating or when you were first married. What were the little things you did for each other that brought you close? You don't have to re-invent the wheel, just rediscover what has worked in the past and put it into practice. Why not set aside a "date" night each week and do something special, just the two of you?

INTIMACY = TIME SPENT
⚬

Intimacy is established by time spent. You cannot buy it in the store. You can't take a pill and know how to be intimate. Many people want intimacy with God, but they only give Him five minutes a day, and that's supposed to counteract 23 hours and 55 minutes with the world. It just doesn't work that way. There is no other way to get intimacy but with time spent.

People say, "I want to trust God. I want to trust my mate. I want to trust my children." Do you know how you learn to trust? You trust *in* intimacy, not before it. People say, "Well, I'll be intimate when I can trust them." No, you must "choose" to be vulnerable to God, to your mate, to your children. In choosing to become intimate and spending time with the Father God, with your mate or children, then trust comes. Trust is not built *before* intimacy. Trust is built *in* intimacy.

If you are alone for whatever reason, you may be saying to yourself, *Well, I don't have anyone with whom to have an intimate relationship.* But God wants you to be intimate with Him and He with you. After all He dwells in you, or at least He wants to dwell in you. Is He? Are you letting Him?

John 15:7 NKJV says, **If you abide in Me, and My words abide in you, you will ask what you desire, and it shall be done for you.** We live IN HIM by choice when we give Him our lives. His Word abides in us also by our choice when we discipline ourselves enough to put His Word into our lives by reading, studying and meditating on it. Then and only then, can we ask what we will.

You are His tabernacle. How much more intimate can you get? Our little Gabrielle says she knows God is living in her heart just by feeling her heart beat — that's being intimate with God!

> Do you not discern and understand that you [the whole church at Corinth] are God's temple (His sanctuary), and that God's Spirit has His permanent dwelling in you [to be at home in you, collectively as a church and also individually]?
>
> 1 Corinthians 3:16

Isaiah 54 speaks of a perpetual covenant of peace God has made with all of us. If we don't have natural children, we can have numerous spiritual children. He says we don't need to be disgraced or ashamed because we are rejected by man, and He will be our spouse. This is true for men and for women because it is a spiritual picture. He is saying there is much for us to do in the body of Christ to bring in the lost, and it doesn't matter if we are married or not in the natural.

Get hooked in to your church body, and find others who need what you have to offer. Develop those spiritual relationships God has waiting for you. Give of yourself with love and time and much will be given back.

> Sing, O barren one, you who did not bear; break forth into singing and cry aloud, you who did not travail with child! For the [spiritual] children of the desolate one will be more than the children of the married wife, says the Lord. Enlarge the place of your tent, and let the curtains of your habitations be stretched out; spare not; lengthen your cords and strengthen your stakes. For you will spread abroad to

the right hand and to the left; and your offspring will possess the nations and make the desolate cities to be inhabited. Fear not, for you shall not be ashamed; neither be confounded and depressed, for you shall not be put to shame. For you shall forget the shame of your youth, and you shall not [seriously] remember the reproach of your widowhood any more. For your Maker is your Husband — the Lord of hosts is His name — and the Holy One of Israel is your Redeemer; the God of the whole earth He is called.

Isaiah 54:1-5

Here's another point I want to make about being alone in the natural sense. You need to love yourself and give to yourself. I was single for a number of years and lived alone. My family was miles away, and I know what it is to be lonely. So don't be afraid to give gifts to yourself and to treat yourself. Go out to dinner. Go buy a special outfit or tickets to a ball game you want to see. Jesus spoke of the greatest commandment in Matthew 22.

You shall love the Lord your God with all your heart, with all your soul, and with all your mind. This is the first and great commandment. And the second is like it: You shall love your neighbor as yourself.

Matthew 22:37-39 NKJV

God would never have said to love your neighbor as yourself if He wanted you to hate yourself. And here's a revelation: you cannot love your neighbor if you don't love yourself. He expects you to love yourself because you are made in His image. And if you don't know how to love yourself, you need to learn how.

One stumbling block to loving ourselves is poor self-image. Do you know that poor self-image is rooted in pride? It doesn't matter whether you are talking good about yourself or bad about yourself, you're still talking about yourself. You are focused on yourself. Whatever you focus on will develop. It's just like a camera. Whatever you focus on is what you get when the picture is developed. Start focusing on God and others, and you won't have time to focus on yourself.

If you struggle with a poor self-image, ask God to show you the root of the problem. You see, if you can get rid of the root, you won't have the problem. Pride is a root to a lot of problems including poor self-image. When you humble yourself before God and realize your image is God's image, you won't have too much problem with pride anymore. Then you can become intimate with Him and with others.

Someone once asked me, "Would you do anything for your children?" I said, "Yes." Then they asked, "But would you do things 'with' your children?" I started asking myself some questions. Is it more important for me to put clothes on their back and food on the table, or is it more important for me to spend time with my children so they understand the value of the clothes and where the food came from? We can miss out by being a provider and not understanding what is most important, spending time with our children and family. We should be doing both — providing and participating — in balance!

MAKE THE FIRST MOVE!

☙

If you are a young person and your dad or mom doesn't spend time with you, then you go spend time with them.

You make the first move. A lot of times Mom and Dad don't spend time with you because they have no idea what to do with you. They think you dress wild, and you think they dress bad. They don't understand where you are coming from, so you go knock on their door and take them out and involve them in your life.

If you want an intimate relationship with them, don't wait until it is too late. Someday they will be gone. My father died when I was only ten, and I missed not having a dad. Anytime I see a father and a son having words, I want to say to them, "I don't care what he did wrong or how mad you are with each other, work it out before the night is over. Tomorrow may be too late."

Do whatever it takes to create more intimacy in your relationship with the Father, with your family and with others of significance in your life. If trust has been broken, then work step-by-step to rebuild that trust. We were created for intimacy. Take back any ground the enemy has stolen, and remember to use your weapons wisely.

> **For though we walk in the flesh, we do not war according to the flesh. For the weapons of our warfare are not carnal but mighty in God for pulling down strongholds, casting down arguments and every high thing that exalts itself against the knowledge of God....**
> **2 Corinthians 10:3-5 NKJV**

Run With Intensity

HARRY SALEM II

Intensity is a critical must for anyone desiring to *be #1 at being #2*. You can't be a couch potato and expect to win. Here is what Paul says about intensity and purpose.

> **Do you not know that in a race all the runners run, but only one gets the prize? Run in such a way as to get the prize. Everyone who competes in the games goes into strict training. They do it to get a crown that will not last; but we do it to get a crown that will last forever. Therefore I do not run like a man running aimlessly; I do not fight like a man beating the air. No, I beat my body and make it my slave so that after I have preached to others, I myself will not be disqualified for the prize.**
>
> **1 Corinthians 9:24-27 NIV**

Run the race to win. And remember winners aren't just the ones who come in first, often winners are those who finish the race! Get up off your chair. Get into training. Go out and do things. I'm not just talking about doing things with your children. Be an example to everyone who enters your sphere of influence each day. Don't just go out and serve food to the homeless on Thanksgiving Day and then not do anything the rest of the year. Be an example every day of your life. Get involved at church in projects and out-reaches. Get to know your neighbors. Develop positive, winning relationships with your boss and co-workers.

How will you get your children away from the TV or Nintendo if you aren't doing it? So, get intense in everything you are doing. Don't let anything stand in your way of fulfilling God's call in your life. The greatest call we can have on our lives is to be an example for the next generation whether it be for our own natural children or for our spiritual children.

Children have their own ways of displaying intensity. One day a boy at school challenged Li'l Harry and said, "If you cross this line, I'll hit you with this rock." Harry responded, "My dad always says, 'Draw a line in the sand and don't go back.'" So he stepped across the line, and the boy hit him in the head with the rock. Several stitches later I asked Harry, "Why did you let this kid hit you with a rock?" He replied with such intensity, "Dad, I couldn't go back!"

We went to the Muppet Show at MGM studios in Orlando. At the very end one of the guys said to one of the Muppets, "Come on down here." The Muppet answered and said, "I'd like to but I'm bolted to the seat, knucklehead." Think about that. Are you bolted to the seat? No, get up, get out, go do!

I remember T. L. Osborn said to me one day, "If you're called, don't stand around mumbling and saying, 'I don't have the money, or I don't know what to do.' If you know you're called, grab a globe, spin it, stick your finger on a spot, and go for it, baby! It's just that simple." It is a simple Gospel. Get up and just do it.

Dr. Roberts says it this way. Find out the will of God. Quit asking for people's opinions, and get it done at all costs. I know you're saying, "But how do I find out the will of God?" Proverbs 16 gives divine direction. It says to commit your ways to Him, commit what you are doing to Him and trust Him. The inner peace you receive will confirm His plans.

> **The plans of the mind and orderly thinking belong to man, but from the Lord comes the [wise] answer of the tongue. All the ways of man are pure in his own eyes, but the Lord weighs the spirits (the thoughts and intents of the heart). Roll your works upon the Lord [commit and trust them wholly to Him; He will cause your thoughts to become agreeable to His will, and] so shall your plans be established and succeed.... When a man's ways please the Lord, He makes even his enemies to be at peace with him.... A man's mind plans his way, but the Lord directs his steps and makes them sure.**
>
> **Proverbs 16:1-3,7,9**

I have heard people say, "God has given me this vision," more times than I can count. Too often that statement is followed by nothing more than talk. Eventually either the vision dies or the opportunity to fulfill the vision passes.

The dreams and visions you have are not going to be accomplished or fulfilled by someone else. You must do what it takes. I had a dream of a wife and family and a career. Cheryl had a dream of being Miss America. I can tell you no one came knocking on my door to see my dream through. Anyone would have been hard pressed to even find Cheryl's house to knock on her door! James 2:20 NKJV says, **Faith without works is dead.** Don't let your vision die. Get up and do something to make it happen.

When God showed Cheryl and me that we were to merge our two callings, our works, we launched out on faith. We did not wait for someone to come knocking. We named the ministry, The Salem Family Ministries, and no longer went in separate directions. We came together on everything. If I had a television shoot, Cheryl was right there. If Cheryl had bookings, I went with her.

Cheryl likes to say, "Our boat had been scraped and the barnacles removed. It was painted and ready to be launched." As we came together, our giftings and anointing began to flow as one, and our boat was launched as a family ministry. When we came in IN-TO-ME-SEE with one another and with God, He made a covenant with us for a new ministry.

You never know where or when your dream or vision is going to come into existence, but you can be sure if you aren't looking you will never find it. Even if your vision is very small, do it with intensity.

The first man on the moon said, "One small step for man, one giant leap for mankind." This was a small physical step, but a huge step forward for technology and America. Actions that may seem small in the natural might be what it takes for something huge to happen in the supernatural. Don't get stuck looking at earthly circumstances. They have limits. Look toward the limitlessness of the supernatural.

Now when Cheryl and I go to minister, we take our children with us as often as we can. Our children sing because they want to be involved. Cheryl plays the piano at home, and they come to her wanting to sing along. We never push it upon them, but when they ask to participate, we make sure they do it the right way and with quality.

When you make things fun and exciting and when you do things with intensity, your children want to do it too. Recently, I was driving along with the three children in the car and suddenly one of the children started singing, "I will enter His gates with thanksgiving in my heart. I will enter His courts with praise." Then another one joined in, "I will say this is the day that the Lord has made." And then the third child joined in with, "I will rejoice for He has made me glad." They continued to sing in unison totally unprompted by me. "He has made me glad. He has made me glad. I will rejoice for He has made me glad...."

My heart was thrilled. Here were my children riding down the road singing to the Lord, praising Him and worshiping Him. It just comes natural to them because they have sung so much with Cheryl. That was the ultimate for me as a father.

When you sound intense about your church, everybody wants to come. When people come out of Disney World, they are excited and say, "I saw this, I saw that, Wow, you should have seen it!" It makes everyone want to go, too. If you come out of church with the same excitement and say, "Boy, this happened and I saw this lady get healed and I got rid of this junk in my life," people will say "What, whoa, wait a minute, I want to hear more about that."

Cheryl and my mother were at the checkout counter at Wal-Mart one day, and the checkout girl was talking with them. Cheryl asked her where she went to church which started a whole conversation about the Lord. You can start conversations with people anywhere with simple questions. Just talk and open the door.

You can sound the call to people everywhere you go. Just be intense about it. Cheryl does this wherever she goes. She says she is instant in season. When we travel to different cities to minister, it isn't unusual for Cheryl to invite ten or fifteen people to the services. These may be bellhops at the hotel or servers at a restaurant or someone she meets at the airport.

People just talk to Cheryl wherever she goes — the grocery store, Wal-Mart, at the hotel pool, in the elevator. They just walk up to her and start talking. I tell her she has a sign on her head that says, "Talk to me!" It's like she shines or glows, and it attracts people to her. Isaiah 60:1 says, **Shine (be radiant with the glory of the Lord), for your light has come, and the glory of the Lord has risen upon you!** I believe people are attracted to the glory of the Lord that shines out of her, and without any prompting they just spill out their life story.

It amazes me sometimes how it happens. On one trip Cheryl made a stop at the ladies' room before boarding the plane. When she came out, she was telling me all about this woman named Margaret she had met. I said, "I would like to meet her, introduce her to me when you see her, okay?" Cheryl said, "I can't." I thought that was strange so I asked her, "Why not?" Cheryl said, "Well, I don't know what she looks like. BUT! She had on blue shoes!" Cheryl never saw the woman's face, but talking through the stall, Margaret shared her life's story. Amazing! I guess even your feet can shine and be radiant for God!!

Intensity is summed up in Matthew 20:16 and 22:14: **For many are called, but few are chosen.** The reason few are chosen is because few are willing to pay the price to be chosen. There is a price to be chosen. It involves integrity. It involves intimacy. It involves intensity.

There is a great price to be paid to follow God, and that price is "everything." It's not paying the price of my wife. "Oh, I'll leave my wife to follow Jesus." No. It's not, "Oh, I'll leave my children and pay the price of my children and follow Jesus." It's not, "I'll pay the price of my job and follow Jesus." No, but "I'll pay the price of 'ME' — my hopes, my dreams, my desires, my wants, my plans, my purposes. I'll pay all of that and sacrifice all of me to have all of Jesus." Jesus said in Matthew 16:24-25:

> **If anyone desires to be My disciple, let him deny himself [disregard, lose sight of, and forget himself and his own interests] and take up his cross and follow Me [cleave steadfastly to Me, conform wholly to My example in living and, if need be, in dying, also]. For whoever is bent on saving his [temporal] life [his comfort and security here] shall lose it [eternal life]; and whoever loses his life [his comfort and security here] for My sake shall find it [life everlasting].**

Now that's intensity. In LIFE there is no "if" in the Great I AM! So get out of the back row and come to the front. Get in the fight. When you are willing to pay the price (of yourself, not someone else!) and deny yourself for the Lord, for your family and for those in your inner circle of life, you will truly *be #1 at being #2*. You will be a servant of the Lord, which we are all called to be.

Taking Inventory

Harry Salem II

Now it's time to take inventory of your life. You understand integrity, intimacy and intensity. With all the things we have talked about, now go back and ask yourself, "Do I have a right father-son relationship? Do I have a right relationship with my mother? Do I have right relationship with my heavenly Father? Am I fulfilling my calling and destiny? What kind of fruit is my life producing?" Take inventory now. Don't wait for a holiday or some event to come along in the future.

One of my close friends was waiting for his parents to arrive on a holiday. He waited and waited. About 5 o'clock that evening, he got a phone call. His parents had been killed in a car wreck on the interstate only a mile and a half from his house. A car came across the median and killed them both.

He had a good relationship with his family, but if he hadn't and had waited to patch it up on that holiday, what would have happened? Don't wait. Get right with your family, with friends and associates.

Most importantly, get right with God. It's not too late and you are worthy. Don't let anyone at school tell you you're not worthy. Don't let anyone at work tell you you're not worthy. And don't let anyone in your family tell you you're not worthy. My Bible says the only way you cannot enter into heaven is by blasphemy, denouncing Jesus Christ. You are worthy.

I think the worst thing we do is to put a guilt trip on everybody by saying, "You're not going to heaven because...." How do we know what is in the heart of someone else? Does the Word say we are to judge or God is to judge? We're going to be very surprised when we get to heaven to see who is there and who isn't there. It is time to take inventory of your life, not someone else's.

First Corinthians 11:28 says, **Let a man [thoroughly] examine himself.** Second Corinthians 13:5 says, **Examine and test and evaluate your own selves.** Galatians 6:4 says, **But let every person carefully scrutinize and examine and test his own conduct and his own work.** You have the right to check yourself. And believe me it's a whole lot easier to examine and test yourself than to have the Lord do it for you.

Look at the Fruit!
❧

Take a good look at yourself and the fruit of your life. Always judge yourself by God's eternal values, not by the values of the world. Every decision we make in our lives should be weighed against eternal values.

Ask yourself these questions. "Is this going to bring any good thing to my future, in my eternal value? Am I making this decision based on something that will have eternal value? Once I cross from this life into eternity will I be glad that I focused on this or will I look back and say, 'Why did I waste my time on that?' What difference will the action resulting from this decision make in my life or someone else's life in the scheme of eternity?"

The movie, *Schindler's List,* was a chilling reality check on what has eternal value. At the end of the movie, Schindler is sitting there looking at his ring and button pondering whether with these two small items he could have gotten ten or even twenty more Jews out of harm's way.

He took inventory of everything he did during those years of war based on how many lives he could save. He risked everything he had and everything he was to save all he could. This made Cheryl and me think about how many more miles we could get out of our van rather than replacing it, so we could spend our money on printing and giving away more children's books to the inner city ministries.

BE ETERNITY CONSCIOUS!

~

We are locked into time consciousness while God is eternity conscious. God sees a long, long never-ending eternity line, and our life on this earth is only a tiny dot on that line. Yet, we spend all of our time in this life learning to live in this earthly, natural realm. We don't comprehend what life will be like in eternity. Cheryl says God has put us on this earth to learn to live heavenly, and if we would learn to live heavenly, we won't have to start from scratch when we reach the heavenly realm.

Don't make this process of examining and testing more difficult than it needs to be. The simplest way is to put it in the light of the Word. If the action resulting from your choices will not bring good fruit, then it isn't worth giving of yourself or your time to do it.

YOU ARE WORTHY!

You are worthy to have a relationship with God and to stand before the Father God, forgiven of all sin and cleansed as white as snow. You have the right to follow the call of God on your life, to sound the call and to heed the call. You have the right to say to your heavenly Father and to Jesus, "IN TO ME SEE." That's your right and opportunity.

You are on this earth to do His work. He is in heaven always interceding for you. He needs you. You need Him. I don't care who you are or where you are. I don't care if you are black, white or brown; if you speak broken English; or if you're divorced; He needs you.

Let me share a story with you. A little boy used to walk by a pet store every day and press his nose up against the window. He would peek in at all the animals, and then he would walk off home. The pet store owner watched him do this day after day while the other kids were out playing.

One day the pet store operator said, "Little boy, why aren't you playing with the other children?" He said, "Oh, no, I don't want to play with the other children." The owner said, "Well, little boy, why don't you come in and get a pet?" The boy said, "No, my daddy says we don't have the money.

146

We can't afford a dog. I think it's something else, but I can't have one."

About three weeks go by and this little boy keeps pressing his nose against the window every day. Finally, the pet store owner invited the little boy in and said, "Come on in here. I want to give you any pet in this store." The little boy said, "Any pet? I'll take a dog." The owner said, "Pick out the one you want." He was tired of seeing that little face pressed up against the window.

The little boy went back to the very back cage and picked out a scrawny, brown dog with braces on its back legs because it was lame. The owner said, "Oh, no, you don't want that dog. You want one that can run in the field with you and jump and play with you." The boy said, "Nope, that's my dog." The owner said, "That dog won't be able to run with you." Then the boy raised up his little pants legs and showed the owner the braces on his legs and said, "See, sir. That's my dog because I can't run or jump or play, and I need that dog and that dog needs me. We need each other."

That's the way God sees you, just like Him in His image. You need God and God needs you. If you're saying to yourself right now, "God, that's me," then pray this prayer: "God, I do need You. I want to heed the call in my life to follow You. I want to have intimacy with You. I give You permission to see into me. I am willing to be vulnerable with You. Teach me how to walk in righteousness and integrity. I want to be intense in heeding my call. I want to be able to do what I am called to do. I want all of You, God, and I willingly give You all of me. I don't know how You can use me, but You do. I put my trust in You, Father. Use me as You will."

A Three-fold Cord

CHERYL SALEM

In all honesty *being #1 at being #2* is a very difficult goal to achieve. The reason is because our human (prideful, self-centered) nature wants to be #1, not #2. It is only when we take on God's humble nature of a servant's heart that we can achieve our goal. During all the struggles in the early years of our marriage and then during the battle with my sickness and depression, Harry and I struggled with these opposing natures. It is a battle everyone faces at home, at work, at church and in every type of relationship. It is a battle that began in the Garden of Eden thousands of years ago, and it is still raging today.

I want to share with you a teaching the Lord gave me as I studied the Word during my illness. I pray it brings you the freedom it has brought to Harry and me. Because of the depth of the truth in this message, you may need to read it more than once and meditate on its meaning. But once you embrace the truth, the battle will no longer rage in your relationships. When you get it down in your spirit, you will find the victory to truly *be #1 at being #2.*

To understand how this battle is fueled, you must understand how God's kingdom principles operate and how Satan's kingdom reacts to these principles. Take notice in the Scriptures how God works in threes starting with the Trinity — Father, Son and Holy Spirit. Three is the number of the Godhead, divine completeness and perfect testimony.[1]

> **So there are three witnesses in heaven: the Father, the Word and the Holy Spirit, and these three are One; and there are three witnesses on the earth: the Spirit, the water and the blood; and these three agree [are in unison; their testimony coincides].**
>
> 1 John 5:8

There were three archangels mentioned in the Word — Michael, Gabriel and Lucifer. Michael, whose name means "who is like God," is believed to be the prince or guardian over the destinies of Israel. He is often referred to as the warring angel. Gabriel whose name means "God is great," is a messenger of God. Lucifer, whose name means "morning star," is believed to have been the archangel of praise who sinned and was thrown out of heaven, thus becoming Satan.[2]

Lucifer's fall was caused by pride. The spirit of pride became so big in him that it was more important to elevate "himself" above God than it was to live in heaven. Pride blinds you to the real truth. Lucifer was so blinded by pride that he actually thought he deserved to be above God. He thought he could accomplish this great rebellious feat in a two-to-one war in heaven — two-thirds of God's angels against his one-third. Any idiot could see the folly of that assumption, but pride is a powerful, deceptive spirit.

When Lucifer (Satan) was thrown out of heaven, he took one-third of the angels with him. They had been under his authority in the ranks of heaven. Satan imitates God's Trinity in every way. Satan knows the Word, and I believe he uses his demonic forces in threes to help accomplish his mission to destroy God's image — us!

Satan counterfeits everything God does. Therefore, the way things "look" with the natural eye is not really the way things are. For example, shyness and timidity may appear to be humility, but they are actually the fear of man, which is pride.

Let's look at how Satan uses the three spirits of pride, blame and shame to counterfeit or pervert three of God's characteristics — humility, wisdom and glory (honor).

It all goes back to the Garden of Eden and the fall of man. God created man in His image with a free will. He gave man dominion over the earth, which elevated man above Satan. You can imagine how mad that made Satan. So Satan came to Eve in the form of a serpent and deceived her into eating from the tree of the knowledge of good and evil. Adam was right there with her watching this event unfold. He wasn't deceived. Adam made a willful choice to disobey God and eat the forbidden fruit. This is where we see pride enter the picture.

> **Pride goes before destruction, and a haughty spirit before a fall. Better it is to be of a humble spirit with the meek and poor than to divide the spoil with the proud.**
>
> **Proverbs 16:18-19**

Immediately upon allowing pride to get a foothold, shame entered the picture, because pride perverts God's glory (or humility) into shame. Adam and Eve saw their nakedness and tried to cover themselves with fig leaves. Pride causes shame to cover or hide your face which closes you off from intimacy and from forgiveness. Adam and Eve hid from God and could no longer walk and talk with Him with the intimacy they experienced before they sinned.

When God asked them why they were hiding, instead of humbly asking for forgiveness, pride raised its ugly head; and shame had a new partner — blame. Adam blamed God for giving him the woman, and then he blamed the woman. This was where the enmity between the genders was birthed. Prior to sinning, man and woman equally shared dominion and authority.

At any point they could have repented, but no! Pride had its ugly tentacles deeply imbedded by now. They were blinded and too busy pointing fingers at and blaming God, each other and the serpent. So judgment was pronounced; and judgment brought more shame, more blame and more pride. With God it's not always the action but the motive behind the action that He is interested in. It wasn't just a matter of eating an apple, He saw Adam and Eve's hearts.

> **For the Lord sees not as man sees; for man looks on the outward appearance, but the Lord looks on the heart.**
>
> **1 Samuel 16:7**

There is strength in numbers. Ecclesiastes 4:12 says, **And though a man might prevail against him who is alone, two will withstand him. A threefold cord is not**

quickly broken. Three single cords or ropes braided together form a rope that is at least three times stronger. Pride, blame and shame are like a three-fold cord or "root" that intertwine. In braiding three strands of hair if you let loose of the center strand, usually the other two loosen up and the braid falls apart. In other words, if we pull down pride, then shame and blame will usually crumble as well. It's the intertwining of the three spirits tightly together that gives the strength to the demonic realm and makes them more difficult to displace.

Satan used the three spirits of pride, shame and blame to steal man's dominion over the earth, to kill (bring death to man spiritually and physically), and to destroy man's intimate relationship with God. He uses many different three-fold combinations of spirits to attack God's people.

Have you ever heard someone say, "Trouble always comes in threes?" It is just evidence of the enemy's rule-of-three tactic. In my life he used the spirits of perfectionism, approval and performance. On the surface not one of these appeared to be bad. They seemed to bring about a good result, but they were all "I" centered — rooted in the spirit of pride — rather than God-centered. Being Miss America opened many doors for spreading the Gospel. My ministry was healing broken hearts and bringing many souls into the kingdom. I had a loving husband and children. But what I was doing wasn't motivated by a pure heart.

The world applauds perfection, the world applauds performance, and the world applauds approval. It doesn't matter to the world if you are "killing yourself" in the process or not honoring your husband or doing everything your way instead of God's way.

I was blinded by pride into thinking I was doing it for God when really I was just feeding those three spirits of perfection, performance and approval. I shared with you in Chapter 5 how Satan almost destroyed my life before God finally got my attention and showed me the truth. All I needed was God's approval, not man's. The truth set me free, and I was able to enter into the Lord's "rest" and find healing and strength.

The spirit of pride is the #1 root spirit used by Satan's destructive forces against God's people. I believe all spirits connected with the spirit of pride bring the curse of death. But be encouraged because where Satan counterfeits, God counteracts. Humility is God's way. Pride is Satan's way. Here's how it works.

- God's spirit of humility, which leads to victory, counteracts Satan's spirit of pride, which leads to destruction!

- God's wisdom, which seeks to shift the glory to God and to someone else, counteracts Satan's spirit of blame, which seeks to blame someone else or pass the guilt on to someone else!

- God's glory or honor, which uncovers the face and opens the heart and the spirit to reflect His light, counteracts Satan's spirit of shame or dishonor, which covers the face and closes off the heart and the spirit with darkness and despair.

Satan uses these three spirits most often to inflict damage to God's kingdom. They are all opposites of God's character. Pride is a mask that is sometimes difficult to see because it has different faces, but it is all the same once you take off the mask. Pride is a covering used to hide something. God's humility is a covering, but it isn't used to hide anything.

Another example of this can be seen in the comparison of God's glory and Satan's shame. God's glory is like a godly coat. Once you put it on, everyone can see the fruit of God's glory shine from you including joy, peace, worthiness, contentment, etc. God's glory opens you up to forgiveness and intimacy with the Father.

Shame is Satan's counterfeit of God's glory; and when you put on the demonic coat of shame, everyone sees the fruit of unworthiness, guilt, despair, rejection, insecurity, etc., all over you. Shame causes you to hide your face and closes you off from forgiveness and intimacy with the Father. That's why Adam and Eve weren't able to repent of their sin in the garden. They were blinded by their shame.

Let's use three different spirits and see how it works.

- God's humility counteracts pride.

- God's wisdom (discipline) counteracts laziness.

- God's prosperity counteracts poverty.

Here's one more example:

- God's intimacy counteracts pride.

- Faith in God counteracts fear.

- God's humility counteracts perversion.

Are you beginning to get the picture? Look at the graphic pictures on pages 197 and 199. See if you can pick out some more groups of three and identify the counterfeits and counteractions. You may find the Scripture references helpful.

Let me introduce Mr. Pride and Mr. Humble. Do you recognize anyone you know? I'm sure you can see that Mr. Humble would be very successful at *being #1 at being #2* while Mr. Pride would be difficult to work for or with.

- Mr. Pride has to have the approval of man. Mr. Humble only needs God's approval and doesn't care what men think.

- Mr. Pride announces himself because he doesn't really know who he is and hopes no one else knows that! Mr. Humble doesn't have to be announced because he knows who he is. He knows he has the favor of God in his life, which ultimately gives him the favor of man, too!

- Mr. Pride has to sit at the head table. Mr. Humble is unconcerned where he sits.

- Mr. Pride is self-centered and easily offended. Mr. Humble is centered on God and hardly notices when done an injustice.

- Mr. Pride is insecure but masked by self-assurance. Mr. Humble is confident and covered in godly assurance.

- Mr. Pride shifts the blame to someone else. Mr. Humble shifts the glory to someone else.

- Mr. Pride says, "I'm somebody. I don't need God. I don't need anybody!" Mr. Humble says, "God doesn't

love me because I'm somebody. I'm somebody because God loves me!"

The Scripture bears witness of Satan's demonic spirits
working in threes. Second Chronicles 20:1 says, **After this,
the Moabites, the Ammonites, and with them the Meunites came against Jehoshaphat to battle.** These were three
ungodly, satanic kingdoms coming against God's people.

The Moabites were controlled by the spirits of pride (ar-
rogance and conceit are part of pride), wrath and lying.

> **We have heard of the pride of Moab, that he is
> very proud — even of his arrogance, his conceit,
> his wrath, his untruthful boasting.**
>
> **But now the Lord has spoken, saying, Within
> three years, as the years of a hireling [who will not
> serve longer than the allotted time], the glory of
> Moab shall be brought into contempt, in spite of
> all his mighty multitudes of people; and the rem-
> nant that survives will be very small, feeble, and of
> no account.**
>
> **Isaiah 16:6,14**

The Ammonites were controlled by the spirits of greed,
jealousy and pride. Both the Moabites and the Ammonites
were established out of the spirit of perversion (incest)
from the sin of Lot's daughters lying with him after they
got him drunk.

> **Because [the Ammonites] have ripped up
> women with child in Gilead, that they might en-
> large their border.**
>
> **Amos 1:13**

> I have heard the taunts of Moab and the revilings
> of the Ammonites by which they have reproached My
> people, and magnified themselves and made boasts
> against their territory. Therefore, as I live, says the
> Lord of hosts, the God of Israel, Moab shall become
> like Sodom and the Ammonites like Gommorah, a
> land possessed by nettles and wild vetches and salt
> pits, and a perpetual desolation. The remnant of My
> people shall make a prey of them and what is left of
> My nation shall possess them. This shall they have
> for their pride, because they have taunted and boast-
> ed against the people of the Lord of hosts.
>
> Zephaniah 2:8-10

The third kingdom which came against Jehoshaphat
was the Meunites from Mt. Seir (Edom is in Seir), and they
were prideful as well. The spirit of Esau (pride), anger and
jealousy ruled over the Meunite people.

> Behold, I will make you small among the na-
> tions [Edom]; you shall be despised exceedingly.
> The pride of your heart has deceived you, you
> dweller in the refuges of the rock [Petra, Edom's
> capital], whose habitation is high, who says in his
> heart, Who can bring me down to the ground?
>
> Obadiah 1:2-3

> Therefore, as I live, says the Lord God, I will
> deal with you according to the anger and envy you
> showed because of your enmity for them, and I will
> make Myself known among them [as He Who will
> judge and punish] when I judge and punish you.
>
> Ezekiel 35:11

Remember it said in Ecclesiastes 4:12 that **a threefold cord is not quickly broken.** Satan knows God's Word, and that is why he attacks in threes — three attacks, three spirits, etc.

Have you noticed when the enemy attacks, he always seems to hit at things that tie together? Those old sayings, "The attack comes from every hand," and "When it rains, it pours," bear witness of this as well. It says in Amos 3:3 NKJV, **Can two walk together, unless they are agreed?** To walk together you must have something in common or have a common bond of some kind.

The common bond between the three demonic spirits sent out against Jehoshaphat and Judah (which means praise) was the spirit of pride. Pride was rampant in all three countries. Once again just like in the Garden of Eden, pride rose up and tried to steal God's praise! But Satan's three-fold cord can be broken by God's three-fold cord in heaven (the Father, the Son and the Holy Spirit), and on the earth (the Word, the blood and the word of our testimony)!

Again we can look at Scripture and see how this was done.

> **Then Jehoshaphat feared, and set himself [determinedly, as his vital need] to seek the Lord; he proclaimed a fast in all Judah.**
>
> **2 Chronicles 20:3**

When you are in trouble, run to God, not away from Him. That is what He wants us to do. He delights in having an intimate, open and honest relationship with us. No trouble is too great for Him.

The people of Judah humbled themselves and asked for God's help. They didn't pretend they could do it themselves.

They fasted. (Fasting is a form of worship and praise.) There was unity among the people. They came seeking the Lord and yearned for Him with *all* their desire. Now that's intimacy!

> **And Judah gathered together to ask help from the Lord; even out of all the cities of Judah they came to seek the Lord [yearning for Him with all their desire].**
>
> **2 Chronicles 20:4**

King Jehoshaphat humbly sought the Lord and prayed, praising God's ability and acknowledging his own inability. He set an example before his people and was intimate with God as well.

> **And Jehoshaphat stood in the assembly of Judah and Jerusalem in the house of the Lord before the new court and said, O Lord, God of our fathers, are You not God in heaven? And do You not rule over all the kingdoms of the nations? In Your hand are power and might, so that none is able to withstand You. Did not you, O our God, drive out the inhabitants of this land before Your people Israel and give it forever to the descendants of Abraham Your friend? They dwelt in it and have built You a sanctuary in it for Your Name, saying, If evil comes upon us, the sword of judgment, or pestilence, or famine, we will stand before this house and before You — for Your Name [and the symbol of Your presence] is in this house — and cry to You in our affliction, and You will hear and save.**
>
> **2 Chronicles 20:5-9**

Jehoshaphat continued reminding God how at His instruction Israel had spared these kingdoms in the past and that these kingdoms now were breaking their vow. It wasn't that God needed to be reminded of all He had done in the past or about this vow being broken. Jehoshaphat was speaking this prayer out loud so the demonic spirits could hear and be reminded of God's mercy and power. He was putting the enemy on notice and reminding them whose land it was and that the people of Judah were not going to give up possession of what God had given them. Then they asked God for instructions on what to do.

That is what you need to do in your prayers when you are in trouble. Put the enemy on notice, stand your ground, and ask the Lord what to do.

> **And now behold, the men of Ammon, Moab, and Mount Seir, whom You would not let Israel invade when they came from the land of Egypt, and whom they turned from and did not destroy — Behold, they reward us by coming to drive us out of Your possession which You have given to us to inherit. O our God, will You not exercise judgment upon them? For we have no might to stand against this great company that is coming against us. We do not know what to do, but our eyes are on You. And all Judah stood before the Lord, with their children and their wives.**
>
> **2 Chronicles 20:10-12**

God heard Jehoshaphat's prayer and answered through a prophet. He encouraged them letting them know it was not their battle but His. Then He gave them specific instructions what to do and even told them where to find the enemy.

> **Hearken, all Judah, you inhabitants of Jerusalem, and you King Jehoshaphat. The Lord says this to you: Be not afraid or dismayed at this great multitude; for the battle is not yours, but God's. Tomorrow go down to them. Behold, they will come up by the Ascent of Ziz, and you will find them at the end of the ravine before the Wilderness of Jeruel. You shall not need to fight in this battle; take your positions, stand still, and see the deliverance of the Lord [Who is] with you, O Judah and Jerusalem. Fear not nor be dismayed. Tomorrow go out against them, for the Lord is with you.**
>
> **2 Chronicles 20:15-17**

Take time to study the specific instructions God gave to King Jehoshaphat and the people of Judah so you can apply these same principles when you are facing a battle. In the next few verses notice what King Jehoshaphat did.

> **And Jehoshaphat bowed his head with his face to the ground, and all Judah and the inhabitants of Jerusalem fell down before the Lord, worshipping Him. And some Levites of the Kohathites and Korahites stood up to praise the Lord, the God of Israel, with a very loud voice.**
>
> **And they rose early in the morning and went out into the Wilderness of Tekoa; and as they went out, Jehoshaphat stood and said, Hear me, O Judah, and you inhabitants of Jerusalem! Believe in the Lord your God and you shall be established;**

believe and remain steadfast to His prophets and you shall prosper.

2 Chronicles 20:18-20

Jehoshaphat was an example to his people. He encouraged them and validated the Word of God. He exhorted their spirit man by speaking faith to them. Unity comes from the head, the leader. If the leader is in unity with God, then the people will be also. This turns people toward God. And they all praised God with a very LOUD voice! They weren't timid or wimpy about it. When he had consulted with the people, he appointed singers to sing to the Lord and praise Him in their holy [priestly] garments as they went out before the army, saying, Give thanks to the Lord, for His mercy and loving-kindness endure forever!

And when they began to sing and to praise, the Lord set ambushments against the men of Ammon, Moab, and Mount Seir who had come against Judah, and they were [self-] slaughtered; for [suspecting betrayal] the men of Ammon and Moab rose against those of Mount Seir, utterly destroying them. And when they had made an end of the men of Seir, they all helped to destroy one another.

2 Chronicles 20:21-23

That's right! They killed each other. Pride is a "self" killer and that is what happened to these prideful kingdoms of Satan. It leads to suicide because it can't deal with failure. Satan's ultimate purpose is to destroy God's image, and he doesn't care how he goes about it. Self-destruction gives him the most pleasure of all. This is further proof to me that the spirit of pride carries with it a curse of death.

The people of Judah did not have to lift a finger and no one was hurt. They were obedient to the Lord, and He fought the battle for them just as He said He would. He will do the same for you and for me if we are obedient and humble ourselves before Him.

Pride is a weapon of destruction, and humility carries a promise of blessings. Just as the armies of the three satanic kingdoms were killed by each other, so the people of Judah received blessings. It took three days to gather all of the spoils of the battlefield after which they all came together and blessed the Lord. The valley where the battle took place was named the Valley of Berachah [blessing]. They returned to Jerusalem with great joy, singing and praising because the Lord had made them to rejoice over their enemies. And they dwelt in peace and rest and safety.

To summarize what we have learned from King Jehoshaphat, let me highlight key points to remember when you find yourself in trouble: run to God, not away from Him; humble yourself and pray; put the enemy on notice; stand your ground; and ask the Lord what to do.

Then use this six-step battle plan when you are facing the enemy's forces. It worked for the people of Judah, and it will work for you because God is the same yesterday, today and forever.

STEP 1: Take the offensive and go out to meet the enemy according to the Lord's instructions. Walk in victory when you are in the midst of your enemies. Have no mercy on Satan or any of his crowd of demons.

STEP 2: Don't be afraid or dismayed. In other words, trust God and release your faith. Declare your faith in Him out loud with your mouth. Use THE POWER OF THE SPOKEN WORD! This is what I began to do a few years ago when Satan had unleashed an all-out attack on my mind, my emotions and my physical body. I said, "Satan, you may harass me with circumstances, situations and symptoms, but you can't make me take the disease OR THE DEFEAT! The battle is not mine, it is the Lord's, and He's already won!"

STEP 3: Stand still and watch God work in your behalf. Don't try to do it for God. He doesn't need your help. He only needs your obedience to believe Him and release your faith in Him!

STEP 4: Praise, dance and worship the Lord in the midst of your enemies. Be bold and be loud. Don't let pride hold you back. Praise is one of the most powerful weapons we have. It confuses and defuses the enemy in his tracks.

STEP 5: Bless the Lord with praises and rejoice over your enemies. Don't try to hide your joy. It is a manifestation of victory.

STEP 6: Enter into His rest. Draw close to Him in that intimate peace He has for you. It is in the intimacy of His presence that you will find rest!

The Lord said in Hosea 4:6, **My people are destroyed for lack of knowledge.** I pray that the revelation and knowledge you have received from this teaching will be life-changing. Satan is a liar and a counterfeit. We don't have to fear him because we have the REAL THING — Jesus Christ! IN HIM we can counteract anything Satan tries to bring our way. Jesus already defeated Satan and destroyed his works. Satan has no legal right or claim to us any longer. His three-fold tactic is nothing more than guerrilla warfare.

> **The reason the Son of God was made manifest (visible) was to undo (destroy, loosen, and dissolve) the works the devil [has done].**
>
> **1 John 3:8**

The war has been won, and it is up to us to enforce the victory of the cross. So don't let the battle continue to rage in your relationships at home, at work, at church or anywhere else. Give Satan his eviction notice. Put on the cloak of God's humility, wisdom and glory and walk in freedom. When you wear God's cloak, you will always *be #1 at being #2.*

Give the Best You Have

CHERYL SALEM

Have you ever asked yourself what is the BEST gift you could give to God? Your spouse? Your family? Your boss? Your friends or associates? Whenever the holidays roll around, we all start thinking about the presents we will buy for everyone. Suppose this year you found yourself with no cash or credit cards? What gifts would you have to give that can't be bought with money?

Then on the other hand, some of us spend more time dreaming about what presents "I" want. How many of you grew up in the days of the Sears *Christmas Wish Catalog*? As a child, did you spend hours studying the pages of toys; or ladies, did you dream of having that beautiful velvet dress; or fellas, were you drooling over all the sports "stuff" and tools?

Harry shared with you in the last few chapters about the "I" "Me" Society in which we live. Americans have been infected with a terrible disease of "I Wants." If we are ever going to be successful at *being #1 at being #2*, this disease of "I Wants" must go.

Our Father God has given us the very best gift anyone could possibly ever give us — His beloved Son, Jesus Christ. Jesus gave us His best gift — His very life! No one took Jesus' life. No one killed Him. He "gave" His life so that we might live forever. It is incomprehensible to me why so many reject this precious gift, but they do. Then the Holy Spirit came to earth to be our gift of comfort and peace, and many, even in the "Church," have rejected Him.

Freely God has given to us — ABUNDANT LIFE, ETERNAL LIFE. All God asks of us in return is that we *believe* and *obey*. Why is that so hard for us to do? To find the answer we must again return to Genesis. We're going to look at the first account of man giving a gift (making an offering) to God. Remember, sin has already entered in, and Adam and Eve have been driven out of the Garden of Eden.

> **And Adam knew Eve as his wife, and she became pregnant and bore Cain; and she said, I have gotten and gained a man with the help of the Lord. And [next] she gave birth to his brother, Abel. Now Abel was a keeper of sheep, but Cain was a tiller of the ground.**
>
> **And in the course of time Cain brought to the Lord an offering of the fruit of the ground. And Abel brought of the firstborn of his flock and of the fat portions. And the Lord had respect and regard for Abel and for his offering. But for Cain and his offering he had no respect or regard. So Cain was exceedingly angry and indignant, and he looked sad and depressed.**
>
> **Genesis 4:1-5**

For years I thought the Lord rejected Cain's offering because it was not a blood sacrifice. But after more careful study, there is more revelation in this passage. It says, In the course of time Cain brought to the Lord an offering of the fruit of the ground. It does not say "the" offering. It says "an" offering.

Look closer at the difference between Cain and Abel's offerings. It says, **Abel brought of the firstborn of his flock and of the fat portions.** The Lord was pleased with Abel's offering because it was his "first" fruit. It was the best of his flock. Cain did not give a "first" fruit offering. He gave "an" offering, and he gave it "in the course of time" or when he got around to it. When he got to the place, where he thought, *Oh yeah, I guess I'd better give "an" offering.* It wasn't anything special. It wasn't his best. That's why God did not respect Cain's offering.

What God is after is not how much it costs, not what works we have done, not the actual sacrifice, because the blood has been shed on Calvary already. What God is after is our "first" fruit of obedience.

> **Samuel said, Has the Lord as great a delight in burnt offerings and sacrifices as in obeying the voice of the Lord? Behold, to obey is better than sacrifice, and to hearken than the fat of rams.**
> **1 Samuel 15:22**

And it's not for God, but for us, so that we can receive all that He has for us. If we don't give "first" fruits, we bring a curse upon ourselves. Cain was cursed not just because he killed Abel but, also, because he did not give his "first" fruit to the Lord.

In our generation the word, "sacrifice," is something we do, but not necessarily something we want to do. But God's definition of sacrifice is to give of our best, to give your "first" fruits, not our "left-over's" or our "I don't want to's." He is looking for our sacrifice of praise. When we give our best with a willing heart, then He will pour out His blessings upon us. But when we try to pass off "second best" or just "an" offering, He will curse our seed — even the seed that is already in the ground!

> **If you will not hear and if you will not lay it to heart to give glory to My name, says the Lord of hosts, then I will send the curse upon you, and I will curse your blessings; yes, I have already turned them to curses because you do not lay it to heart. Behold, I will rebuke your seed [grain — which will prevent due harvest], and I will spread the dung from the festival offerings upon your faces, and you shall be taken away with it.**
>
> **Malachi 2:2-3**

In Chapter 5 I shared with you how I would do what Harry told me to do, but I was sputtering and muttering to myself every step of the way. I was sitting down on the outside but standing up on the inside. To all outward appearances I was a submissive, obedient wife. But in truth I was exhibiting Satan's counterfeit, the exact opposite — rebellion. My heart wasn't pure and God could not bless my marriage relationship. I wasn't planting good seed so I wasn't reaping the harvest I wanted to receive.

We must understand how God's kingdom operates. He has established certain spiritual laws, and He will not violate these laws for any reason. To go against His own laws and principles would be to deny His own character. The law of sowing and reaping is just such a law. The only way you can live a life of blessing — *being #1 at being #2* — is to first walk in obedience to the Lord.

Let's explore more about God's methods of operation. We can learn so much from the Israelites' journey in the wilderness.

> **For the Israelites walked forty years in the wilderness till all who were men of war who came out of Egypt perished, because they did not hearken to the voice of the Lord; to them the Lord swore that He would not let them see the land which the Lord swore to their fathers to give us, a land flowing with milk and honey.**
>
> **So it was their uncircumcised children whom He raised up in their stead whom Joshua circumcised, because the rite had not been performed on the way. When they finished circumcising all the males of the nation, they remained in their places in the camp till they were healed. And the Lord said to Joshua, This day have I rolled away the reproach of Egypt from you. So the name of the place is called Gilgal [rolling] to this day.**
>
> **Joshua 5:6-9**

In examining this passage we see that Egypt is representative of "not enough." The wilderness is representative of "just enough," and Caanan is representative of "more than enough." The word "reproach" means shame, disgrace and guilt.[1] So the Scripture passage could read like this, "This

171

day have I taken away the shame, disgrace and guilt of not having enough."

Isaiah 10:27 NKJV says, **It shall come to pass in that day That his burden** [of the Assyrian] **will be taken away from your shoulder, And his yoke from your neck, And the yoke will be destroyed because of the anointing oil.** The yoke is destroyed because of the anointing!

So the anointing of God is the burden-removing, yoke-destroying power of God. What does the word "Christ" mean? It means "the anointed one."[2] Therefore, Christ, the Anointed One, is the burden-removing, yoke-destroying power of God!

The apostle Paul speaks of Christ's bountiful supply.

> **For I am well assured and indeed know that through your prayers and a bountiful supply of the Spirit of Jesus Christ (the Messiah) this will turn out for my preservation (for the spiritual health and welfare of my own soul) and avail toward the saving work of the Gospel.**
>
> **Philippians 1:19**

So what is this bountiful supply of the Spirit of Jesus Christ? It is anything we need — healing, restoration, redemption, finances, salvation. Whatever we need, God has a bountiful supply.

El Shaddai, one of the names of God, means "more than enough" or "many breasted one."[3] When a demand is made upon a breast to continue to supply milk, it will automatically produce more and more milk until the demand decreases or stops altogether. As long as there is a demand, there is always a bountiful supply! God's nature is just like His name. In fact, He is this! The many breasted one continues to meet the demands of our needs with a bountiful supply.

> **And you Philippians yourselves well know that in the early days of the Gospel ministry when I left Macedonia, no church (assembly) entered into partnership with me and opened up [a debit and credit] account in giving and receiving except you only. For even in Thessalonica you sent [me contributions] for my needs, not only once but a second time. Not that I seek or am eager for [your] gift, but I do seek and am eager for the fruit which increases to your credit [the harvest of blessing that is accumulating to your account]. But I have [your full payment] and more; I have everything I need and am amply supplied, now that I have received from Epaphroditus the gifts you sent me. [They are the] fragrant odor of an offering and sacrifice which God welcomes and in which He delights. And my God will liberally supply (fill to the full) your every need according to His riches in glory in Christ Jesus.**
>
> Philippians 4:15-19

Almost everyone can quote verse 19, **And my God will liberally supply (fill to the full) your every need,** but how many times have you heard the previous verses quoted? Not too often, and yet verse 19 only works when the previous verses have been acted upon also.

In other words, you can't draw out of an account unless you have made a deposit. You can't get money out of your checking account unless you have first deposited some money into it. This is how God's debit and credit system works. This is His planting and reaping system. You can't drink from a glass unless you first put some water into it. You can't harvest where nothing has been planted.

In verse 19 to whom was Paul referring when he said, **And my God will liberally supply your every need?** The "your" was referring to the Philippians to whom Paul was writing the letter. The Philippians had entered into partnership with Paul and opened up an account in giving and receiving with God's anointed one and His anointing!

When you are a giver, you have the right to believe God will supply all of your needs, but if you have not put anything into the account, there won't be anything to draw out. This Scripture does not apply to you until you enter into a partnership of giving and receiving in the kingdom of God, God's method of operating, God's way of doing things.

You might be saying, "But God, my needs are so great I can't make it to the end of the month much less enter into a giving and receiving partnership. I have nothing left to deposit." The answer is very simple. Before you spend one thin dime, give "first" into God's partnership account. It's the only way! Remember how God respected Abel's "first" fruits offering and despised Cain's offering.

You may be thinking, *But you can't imagine the needs I have!* I may not be able to imagine, but God can. You may have a lot of such thoughts but don't let any of them take root in your thinking. As Kenneth Hagin says, "You may not be able to stop the birds from flying over your head, but you sure can stop them from building a nest in your hair." You see, God already knows what your needs are, and He wants you to make "an acceptable" offering so He can bless you.

This is not just speaking of giving financially. It speaks of whatever you give to others. It may be a smile or speaking forth words of hope and encouragement. You may sow love and peace into a situation where turmoil has reigned. Your prayers for others are a gift.

Paul was excited about the Philippian's fruit which was theirs as a result of their giving. He knew they were laying up treasures in heaven that had eternal value. We need to make our decisions about giving based on eternal value, not what's in it for us.

> But gather and heap up and store for yourselves treasures in heaven, where neither moth nor rust nor worm consume and destroy, and where thieves do not break through and steal; for where your treasure is, there will your heart be also.
>
> Matthew 6:20-21

When we truly learn how to operate by God's principles, we will find our needs being met and then some. In our natural, earthly minds we get the cart before the horse so to speak. When we operate by eternal values and seek God's way first, then we will find His rewards.

> Therefore do not worry and be anxious, saying, What are we going to have to eat? or, What are we going to have to drink? or, What are we going to have to wear? For the Gentiles (heathen) wish for and crave and diligently seek all these things, and your heavenly Father knows well that you need

**them all. But seek (aim at and strive after) first of
all His kingdom and His righteousness (His way of
doing and being right), and then all these things
taken together will be given you besides.**

Matthew 6:31-33

Sometimes we don't receive all God has for us because
we don't believe in God's methods of doing things. In other
words, we let unbelief and doubt cloud our minds instead of
standing in faith. Even the disciples had to learn this lesson.

**Because of the littleness of your faith [that is,
your lack of firmly relying trust]. For truly I say to
you, if you have faith [that is living] like a grain of
mustard seed, you can say to this mountain, Move
from here to yonder place, and it will move; and
nothing will be impossible to you.**

Matthew 17:20

It wasn't the size of their faith that was the problem.
They weren't treating their faith like a seed, a living or live
seed. How can we treat our faith like a living seed? First of
all, we must plant it in our hearts and water it with the Word
of God. Then we must cultivate and fertilize it with positive,
God-filled words! At all times we must protect it — pull out
all the weeds (negative words). Lastly, we must wait on it to
grow and mature.

Remember how God created this world. He had faith
like a seed. He had faith in what He said. In Genesis 1 we
read over and over, "And God said..., And God said..., And
God said..., And God saw...." What did God see? He saw
what He said even before it was created! This is God's way

176

of doing things. Words are powerful instruments of faith-producing results.

> **By faith we understand that the worlds [during the successive ages] were framed (fashioned, put in order, and equipped for their intended purpose) by the word of God, so that what we see was not made out of things which are visible. [Prompted, actuated] by faith Abel brought God a better and more acceptable sacrifice than Cain, because of which it was testified of him that he was righteous [that he was upright and in right standing with God], and God bore witness by accepting and acknowledging his gifts. And though he died, yet [through the incident] he is still speaking.**
>
> **Hebrews 11:3-4**

Faith is in the Word of God. The Word of God is the substance of things hoped for. In other words, living by faith is living by the Word of God. They are synonymous, interchangeable, the same! If you plant God's Word like a seed in your life, treat it like a seed, water, cultivate, fertilize and protect it; you will watch it grow and produce a harvest in your life.

The kingdom of God is not natural or logical. The smallest seed grows into the largest of trees.

> **With what can we compare the kingdom of God, or what parable shall we use to illustrate and explain it? It is like a grain of mustard seed, which, when sown upon the ground, is the smallest of all seeds upon the earth: Yet after it is sown, it grows up and becomes the greatest of all garden herbs**

**and puts out large branches, so that the birds of the
air are able to make nests and dwell in its shade.**
Mark 4:30-32

A seed grows up and becomes much substance, which
then has many more seeds in it for you to plant! When you
seek God's kingdom way of doing things — seedtime and
harvesttime — you will be able to make an acceptable offering to the Lord and reap all of His benefits and blessings.
God will take your smallest of seeds and multiply it into the
largest of harvests.

Think carefully about what you have to give away to
others. This quote from Zig Ziglar says it so well, "Among
the things you can give and still keep are your word, a smile,
and a grateful heart."[4]

Give according to your ability to give, always with an attitude of gratitude, and remember the things of greatest
value can't be measured by their cost. Give your "most acceptable" offering — the BEST you have to give — every day,
and you will truly *be #1 at being #2.*

CHAPTER 17

Learning to Learn

HARRY SALEM II

From the moment we are born until the moment we die, we never stop learning. God created us with the five senses of sight, hearing, taste, touch and smell with which to experience the gift of life. Therefore, learning often is an unconscious effort by which we gain knowledge through experience such as a baby learning to cry for food.

Life is an ever changing kaleidoscope of learning. It is what we do with what we learn that determines our laughter or tears, our successes or failures, our victories or defeats.

Not long ago I was with T. L. Osborn, and he was asked how he just seems to keep going on after losing his beloved wife, Daisy. He said, "I'm learning to learn each and every day." Even at his age and experience in life, he is willing to keep on learning from everybody and every situation.

When a small child who is told repeatedly not to touch a hot burner because it is "hot" touches the burner anyway and feels the pain associated with "hot," he usually learns not to touch the burner again. However, the next time he is told not to touch some other object because it is "hot," he may or may not choose to heed the warning.

What we do with what we learn is a matter of choice. The smartest person in a room is the person who is always willing and seeking to learn something from others and from the circumstances and events that happen around them. It doesn't matter if you are five years old or eighty-five years old, you can gain knowledge from any person and any situation.

There are many different ways to learn — study, instruction, experience, etc. Some people learn more quickly by what they see, and others learn more easily by what they hear. No one way is better than another. God made each of us unique to use the senses and gifts He has given us in different ways.

Cheryl and I have been so blessed to travel and meet people from all over the world and from all walks of life. I pick up little nuggets from people everywhere I go. It is amazing how many little nuggets of wisdom get dropped in your heart if you pay attention and don't take them for granted. I say I have been mentored by the world, not to be "worldly" but to be "godly." There have been key times when I have been at just the right place at the right time to learn from other people's mistakes and situations. You could not have worked in the ministry over the past seventeen years and have seen what I have seen — the good times and the hard times people have gone through — and not learn from those experiences.

I believe the Lord is saying to Cheryl and me in our ministry, "Don't get on the band wagon, lead the band." We don't have to duplicate what others do! We have been mentored by so many great people, and the Lord is saying, "Go out and apply the *best* of what you have learned."

One way we will do that is by setting our values higher than our goals. When we first set high eternal values, our goals will far exceed what we can imagine. You see, if you set goals and you don't have an eternal value system, you will compromise your values for your goals. You cannot overachieve or outdo a goal system.

I could have set a goal to be a millionaire and made money in a number of different areas. But what would it have cost my family? How would I have had to compromise my values to achieve such a goal? Many people have prostituted themselves by sacrificing their values for their goals. I believe you have to be true to yourself and true to your value system. If you can't be true to both, then you are in the wrong place.

I shared in an earlier chapter how as a little boy I chose Rosie Grier to be my role model. A few years after joining the Roberts' Ministry, I was in Los Angeles doing some television specials, and Rosie was one of the guests. How many people actually get to meet their role model? We not only met and had lunch, but we also struck up a friendship that has lasted to this day.

Rosie was just like I thought he would be. He was kind in heart, tender in talk, sweet in spirit, the nicest guy you would ever want to meet — a 250-plus pound good guy! It made me think about my attitude and relationships with people. I began to realize that I could be tough and tender too. Rosie Grier is a living example of that balance.

Over the next few years, I had the pleasure of spending time with Rosie on several occasions. One time I had to pick him up at the airport. The night before I had left the sunroof open on my Honda, and it had rained. I had put a towel in my seat earlier that morning, but I didn't think about the other seat being wet as I drove to the airport to pick him up.

Imagine Rosie Grier getting into a Honda Prelude! He managed to squeeze himself in and at first didn't say anything. As I got on the expressway he said, "Harry, man, you've got to get a sedan or something!" I told him that maybe God would provide me with a nice big sedan just for him by the time he came again. It was quiet for a moment. Then he mumbled, "Well, while you're asking God for a new sedan, ask Him for one with dry seats!"

A couple of years later, Rosie came to town again and saw Cheryl and me talking. He was surprised to see that I knew her. I explained that I knew her quite well as we had been married for a month. It turned out Cheryl had met Rosie and his wife, Margie, and spent time with them after she won Miss America. They were good friends. God surely had His hand on Cheryl and me both to give us such wonderful, godly people to have as friends and role models.

It is unfortunate but in our society I believe the word "hero" has been changed to "idol." I think the worst thing society has done is to take someone like a professional athlete and made him god-like. The worst thing they have done is take a well-known minister and made him god-like. When Satan wanted to be god-like, it was his end. So, don't ask me to put someone up as a hero, because they are just men and women with faults and weaknesses, just like me.

This may sound prideful and I don't mean it to sound that way. I believe God puts people in our lives from whom we can learn specific knowledge or truths. Role model or mentor is a more appropriate title, and we should categorize them as business mentors, family mentors, ministry mentors. I admire different people for specific giftings or qualities they exhibit.

Cheryl prays over our children each day by paraphrasing Proverbs 18:16, "Your gift will make room for you and bring you before great men." They may be role models for others someday as their gift makes room for them and others see it.

I once wrote a letter to President Reagan, and I got a letter back from him with a handwritten note. I keep it still today because I felt he was a person who came in and waved the American flag and supported what America was supposed to be. He was a unique man in a time when no one trusted politicians. His work ethic called for rebuilding America from Americans through Americans. He formed committees and brought people out of the workforce to get things done.

In ministry I look at the integrity of the Roberts, Dr. Lester Sumrall, the Hagins, the Humbards and the Copelands. They raised their children up with them in the ministry, not without them. As a result as far as I could tell, their children didn't grow up hating or despising the ministry.

Here are some of the qualities I have learned from specific people. My mother has the quality of love. Dr. Roberts has the quality of obedience and sacrifice. Cheryl has the quality of faith and has been an example to me.

Desire is a quality all of them have had. My mom had the desire to serve our family through love and to see each of her children serving the Lord. Oral had the desire to serve God through his obedience. Cheryl had the desire to serve God through her testimony.

Desire is a passion or a love or a calling — something you want to do more than anything else. Desire is a drive that pushes people to the edge where nothing else matters. It can be dangerous when someone doesn't have any foundation in the Lord or has a weakness in some area of their life. That is exactly where Satan will attack them.

To fulfill a desire or calling requires a "never-give-up" attitude. Look at President Reagan. Someone tried to kill him, but he just continued on. No matter how much the world attacked him, Oral just wouldn't give up. T. L. Osborn lost the love of his life, but he hasn't given up. They all continue on because no matter how successful they have become, they are still learning to learn.

Jesus was the greatest teacher of all time. He honored His Father and only did what He saw His Father do. In obedience He learned what it was like to walk as a man. He experienced everything that we experience on this earth.

Jesus knew the value of mentorship. He carefully chose His twelve disciples and that included Judas Iscariot. He didn't choose them just because He was lonely and didn't want to be alone. He had a specific purpose for them to fulfill.

And He went up on the mountain and called to Him those He Himself wanted. And they came to Him. Then He appointed twelve, that they might

> **be with Him and that He might send them out to**
> **preach, and to have power to heal sicknesses and**
> **to cast out demons.**
>
> **Mark 3:13-14 NKJV**

He invested His time and His life in them. He equipped them and then sent them out to duplicate His teaching and His life. He gave us a model to follow.

Carefully select your associates. Surround yourself with men and women who honor God's principles, demonstrate His success *and* share your vision and purpose. Give of yourself to both learn from and disciple those "God places" in your circle of influence, including your family, friends, neighbors, business associates, church acquaintances, etc. Invest quality and quantity time in them just as Jesus did — in groups and one-on-one.

Jesus' brilliance as a teacher is recorded in the gospels in parables and words of insight and wisdom that apply to our lives today just as they did in His day. The "wisdom of the ages" is revealed in His Word — the greatest history book and textbook ever written. Look at how successful His disciples were in carrying out His instructions and in fulfilling His commission even after He left them.

Whenever you are at a loss for how to train those around you or how to solve an impossible problem, turn to His Word. The answer is right at your fingertips.

A Christian couple once shared that they never leave the house without asking the Lord what teaching He would have them to share if the opportunity arises. If they are on their way to go shopping or to a ball game with their children or even to church, they ask each other what the Lord has shown them that day. They are "instant in season" with their words of wisdom and insight. As a result they have become two of the most anointed teachers of God's Word I have ever known. The best way to learn is to teach others.

The most effective teacher or mentor will always look for ways to demonstrate and apply the principles being taught. This is why Jesus taught in parables so the people could see the application in day-to-day situations. He was patient in explaining the meaning of His teaching if they didn't understand it the first time. In Matthew 13 Jesus taught the multitudes the parable of the sower and the parable of the wheat and the tares. After He finished teaching here is what happened.

> **Then Jesus sent the multitude away and went into the house. And His disciples came to Him, saying, "Explain to us the parable of the tares of the field." He answered and said to them: "He who sows the good seed is the Son of Man. The field is the world, the good seeds are the sons of the kingdom, but the tares are the sons of the wicked one. The enemy who sowed them is the devil, the harvest is the end of the age, and the reapers are the angels. Therefore as the tares are gathered and burned in the fire, so it will be at the end of the age."**
>
> **Matthew 13:36-40 NKJV**

He patiently repeated His teaching in greater depth with explicit explanations. He even gave them three more parables to consider — the hidden treasure, the pearl of great price and the parable of the dragnet. Then He verified their understanding of what He had taught them. When those around us are hungry, we should always be ready to feed them a little more.

> **Jesus said to them, "Have you understood all these things?" They said to Him, "Yes, Lord." Then He said to them, "Therefore every scribe instructed concerning the kingdom of heaven is like a householder who brings out of his treasure things new and old."**
>
> **Matthew 13:51-52**

We see this repeated again in Mark 4:33-34 NKJV: **And with many such parables He spoke the word to them as they were able to hear it. But without a parable He did not speak to them. And when they were alone, He explained all things to His disciples.**

Never assume everyone understands what you have told them. Ask questions and from the responses you get you will know if you were understood. This is important with children and adults. Be careful not to embarrass someone who doesn't understand you the first time. You may need to take them aside and talk with them one-on-one.

Jesus also knew that His disciples had to step out and practice what He was teaching them even if it meant failing at times. The disciples unsuccessfully tried to deliver a mute boy who had terrible convulsions, but they were not able to cast the spirit out of him. Jesus then spoke with the boy's father and cast the spirit out. When they were alone, he explained why they were not successful. It was because they had not prepared themselves and obtained the anointing.

> **And when He had come into the house, His**
> **disciples asked Him privately, "Why could we not**
> **cast it out?" So He said to them, "This kind can**
> **come out by nothing but prayer and fasting."**
>
> **Mark 9:28-29 NKJV**

As difficult as it is sometimes, we have to let those we are teaching test their wings. That is particularly difficult with our children and even sometimes with our spouse. If we don't let them try, they will never gain confidence and learn what works and what doesn't work. They have to "do it" themselves. Experience is the best teacher.

There is so much we can learn from Jesus' teaching style and principles. Another very important principle was that He never sent them out alone. He knew the power of two and the danger of attacks from their enemy — the devil.

> **Two are better than one, because they have a**
> **good reward for their labor. For if they fall, one will**
> **lift up his companion. But woe to him who is alone**
> **when he falls, for he has no one to help him up.**
> **Again, if two lie down together, they will keep**
> **warm; but how can one be warm alone? Though one**
> **may be overpowered by another, two can withstand**
> **him. And a threefold cord is not quickly broken.**
>
> **Ecclesiastes 4:9-12 NKJV**

We can learn a great deal from the animal kingdom. Did you know that a lion will never attack an animal that is part of a herd? A lion will watch and wait until an animal falls behind or wanders off away from the herd alone. Then he will move in for the kill. It is similar to the "divide and conquer" battle technique used in warfare down through the ages. Jesus knew how Satan operates and how important it was for the disciples to work together.

> **Be well balanced (temperate, sober of mind), be vigilant and cautious at all times; for that enemy of yours, the devil, roams around like a lion roaring [in fierce hunger], seeking someone to seize upon and devour.**
>
> **1 Peter 5:8**

So, Jesus sent out His disciples two by two and gave them specific, detailed instructions. He also warned them of what difficulties to expect, equipping them for the battles they would face.

> **After these things the Lord appointed seventy others also, and sent them two by two before His face into every city and place where He Himself was about to go. Then He said to them, "The harvest truly is great, but the laborers are few; therefore pray the Lord of the harvest to send out laborers into His harvest. Go your way; behold I send you out as lambs among wolves."**
>
> **Luke 10:1-3 NKJV**

It is important to note that ALL seventy returned. They all had obeyed and followed His plan. They had gotten their feet wet and were they ever excited. Jesus exhorted and cautioned them at the same time. He rejoiced with them and gave thanks to the Father. The word "rejoice" translated means "whirled around."[1] That's how excited Jesus was.

> **Then the seventy returned with joy, saying, "Lord, even the demons are subject to us in Your**

name." And He said to them, "I saw Satan fall like lightning from heaven. Behold, I give you the authority to trample on serpents and scorpions, and over all the power of the enemy, and nothing shall by any means hurt you. Nevertheless do not rejoice in this, that the spirits are subject to you, but rather rejoice because your names are written in heaven."

In that hour Jesus rejoiced in the Spirit and said, "I thank You, Father, Lord of heaven and earth, that You have hidden these things from the wise and prudent and revealed them to babes. Even so, Father, for so it seemed good in Your sight."

Luke 10:17-21 NKJV

Whether we are being mentored or are mentoring someone else, all of these principles are critical for success. Jesus was a master communicator, and we need to be as well.

A friend shared this example of how a five-year-old son taught his father a lesson in communication. The father was working on his car and his little boy wanted to help. After checking the radiator and adding some needed antifreeze, the father picked up the hose to add just a little more water.

He stationed his son next to the faucet and turned the water on just a little bit. When the radiator was just about full, he told his son to turn off the water quickly. Instead of turning the faucet off, the little boy turned the knob the wrong way which sent a flood of water into the radiator diluting the antifreeze and splashing water and antifreeze all over his father.

The father's immediate reaction was one of frustration and anger. He turned on his son with the hose and said, "I told you to turn the water OFF!" As the father and son stood there dripping wet, the son said with tears in his eyes, "But Daddy, you didn't teach me how to turn the faucet off!"

With tears in his own eyes, the father got down on his knees and asked his son to forgive him for being angry and not teaching him how to do what he was asking him to do. This father was still learning.

Our heavenly Father places great value on wisdom. The book of Proverbs is filled with great revelations on wisdom.

> **My son, if you receive my words, and treasure my commands within you, so that you incline your ear to wisdom, and apply your heart to understanding; yes, if you cry out for discernment, and lift up your voice for understanding, if you seek her as silver and search for her as for hidden treasures; then you will understand the fear of the Lord, and find the knowledge of God.**
>
> **For the Lord gives wisdom; from His mouth come knowledge and understanding; He stores up sound wisdom for the upright; He is a shield to those who walk uprightly; He guards the paths of justice, and preserves the way of His saints. Then you will understand righteousness and justice, equity and every good path.**
>
> **Proverbs 2:1-9 NKJV**

It is our choice to walk in wisdom. If we will humble ourselves and walk uprightly IN HIM, there is nothing He will withhold from us. If we incline ourselves to His instruction, we will be able to fulfill our calling. We must continuously be learning to learn.

In Weakness We Become Strong

HARRY AND CHERYL SALEM

We could all live our lives in the realm of "what if's," but God has a better way. He has called us and redeemed us. He has promised we won't drown and we won't be burned. No matter where we walk, He is with us, and He is our Savior.

> **Fear not, for I have redeemed you; I have called you by your name; you are Mine. When you pass through the waters, I will be with you; and through the rivers, they shall not overflow you. When you walk through the fire, you shall not be burned, nor shall the flame scorch you. For I am the Lord your God, The Holy One of Israel, your Savior.**
>
> **Isaiah 43:1-3 NKJV**

His desire for us is to close the door on the past and look forward into the bright and shining future of His promises.

> **Do not remember the former things, nor consider the things of old. Behold, I will do a new thing, now it shall spring forth; shall you not know**

> it? I will even make a road in the wilderness and
> rivers in the desert.
>
> **Isaiah 43:18-19** NKJV

We praise the Lord for what He has taken us out of, for where we are today and for where He is taking us in the future. In our testimony you have read how we walked through the floods of depression and near death and the fire of having a two-headed monster in our home that could easily have brought destruction to our family.

But our God was faithful and never let us down. He carried us when we needed to be carried and through our weaknesses He made us strong. We truly can relate to what the apostle Paul wrote.

> **And He said to me, "My grace is sufficient for you, for My strength is made perfect in weakness." Therefore most gladly I will rather boast in my infirmities, that the power of Christ may rest upon me. Therefore I take pleasure in infirmities, in reproaches, in needs, in persecutions, in distresses, for Christ's sake. For when I am weak, then I am strong.**
>
> **2 Corinthians 12:9-10** NKJV

We don't desire to ever again have to walk where we have walked these past few years, but we can truthfully say we are glad we did walk there. The rewards have been worth all the pain.

Our marriage is stronger and more fulfilling than ever before now that we truly have one head and one heart. We are experiencing the joy and peace of having a more intimate relationship with our heavenly Father, with each other, and with our children.

We are seeing the fruit of planting eternal values in our children as they are discovering their own pieces of the puzzle in our family ministry and are filling out their own shoes to the tiptoes.

We are learning more and more how to trust our Savior (Jehovah Jireh) for our daily provision as we sow richly into His kingdom with the best we have to give.

We have not arrived where we want to be or need to be, but we are learning to learn day by day as we lean more on Him and less on ourselves. It is an exciting time to be a part of the body of Christ. We are going where God calls us and loving the people He puts in our path.

We pray that the wisdom we have shared in this book will bring you out of darkness and into the light of God's love. Grab onto the three-fold cord of God's humility, wisdom and glory and don't let go.

Ask Him to show you areas of deception where your belief system may have been twisted by generational curses or judgments and determine in your heart to find the truth.

Build your life and your family on the Rock of Jesus Christ and His eternal values. Purpose in your heart to give the best you have to the Lord and to others around you.

Search out God's wisdom in His Word and in the godly counsel of others God places in your path. And then keep on learning to learn day by day.

As you diligently pursue *being #1 at being #2*, the Lord will surely bring blessing and promotion in every area of your life.

May the Lord bless you and make His light to shine upon you. We love you!

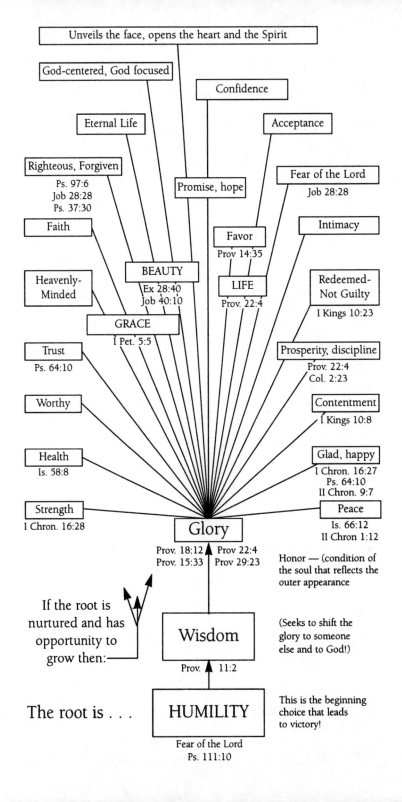

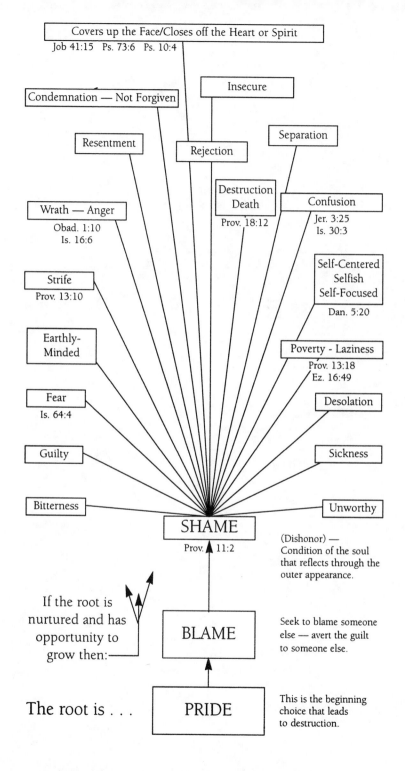

Endnotes

Chapter 5
[1] Evans, Session 1, p. 2.

Chapter 6
[1] Rodale, pp. 1184-1185.

Chapter 7
[1] Finzel.

Chapter 10
[1] Sheets.

Chapter 11
[1] Dear Abby.
[2] Webster, p. 1156.

Chapter 15
[1] Conner, p. 53.
[2] *Nelson's Illustrated Bible Dictionary.*

Chapter 16
[1] *Strong's Hebrew and Chaldee Dictionary,* p. 44.
[2] *Strong's Greek Dictionary of the New Testament,* p. 78.
[3] *Strong's Hebrew and Chaldee Dictionary,* p. 112.
[4] Ziglar, p. 85.

Chapter 17
[1] *Strong's Greek Dictionary of the New Testament,* p. 7.

References

Conner, Kevin J. *Interpreting the Symbols and Types*. Bible Temple Publishing, Portland: Oregon, 1992.

Dear Abby. *Mother Shares ABC's of Successful Parenting*. Tulsa World, Tulsa, Oklahoma.

Evans, Jimmy. *Dream Marriage: Creating Your Dream Marriage Through God's Principles*. Seminar Manual, Session 1.

Finzel, Hans. *The Top Ten Mistakes Leaders Make*.

Nelson's Illustrated Bible Dictionary. Biblesoft: PC Study Bible for Windows, Thomas Nelson Publishers, 1986.

Rodale, J. I. *The Synonym Finder*. Warner Books Edition, Rodale Press Inc., New York: New York, 1978.

Sheets, Dutch. *Why We Should Persevere*. Sermon tape, Sojourn Church, Carrollton, Texas, 1997.

Strong, James. *The Exhaustive Concordance of the Bible*. Hendrickson, Peabody, Massachusetts.

Webster's New World Dictionary. 3rd College Ed. Prentice Hall, New York: New York, 1994.

Ziglar, Zig. *Something to Smile About*. Thomas Nelson Publishers, Nashville: Tennessee, 1997.

About the Authors

Harry A. Salem II grew up in Flint, Michigan. After his father's death in 1968 he relocated with his family to Florida. In 1980, he joined the Oral Roberts Ministry and at the age of 26 became Vice President of Operations and Crusade Director. In his work as author, television writer, producer and director he has won several Angel and Addy Awards. Harry stepped out of his roles at ORU when he and his wife began ministering together.

Cheryl Salem grew up in Choctaw County, Mississippi, and overcame many challenges to become Miss America 1980. She is an accomplished author, speaker, musician, song writer and teacher. She has recorded over seven music titles and written several best sellers. She co-hosts *Make Your Day Count,* shown daily across the nation.

Harry and Cheryl formed Salem Family Ministries which focuses on family, relationships, and overcoming depression and abuse. Together they have written over 15 books including *An Angel's Touch,* which is already in its second printing and is also in the top 25 Best Sellers for 1997. *For Men Only* and *Warriors of the Word* reached combined sales of nearly 10,000 copies last year. Orders are pouring in for the Salem's newest release on overcoming depression, *It's Too Soon To Give Up.*

Their ministry spread to Holland this year where they participated in the European Broadcasting Organization's special on Angels. This year they have nearly 100 ministering opportunities already scheduled.

When not in their home in Tulsa, Oklahoma, they continue to minister full time throughout the world with their three children, Harry III, Roman and Gabrielle.